The Librarian's
NITTY-GRITTY GUIDE TO
SOCIAL MEDIA

ALA Editions purchases fund advocacy, awareness, and accreditation programs for library professionals worldwide.

The Librarian's
NITTY-GRITTY GUIDE TO
SOCIAL MEDIA

LAURA SOLOMON

An imprint of the American Library Association

Chicago   2013

Laura Solomon is library services manager for the Ohio Public Information Network and former web applications supervisor for the Cleveland Public Library. She has been doing web development and design and conducting classes in public libraries and as an independent consultant for more than a decade. In 2009, the Ohio Library Council recognized her for her role in saving more than $147 million of public library funding by utilizing her expertise in social media tools. She was tapped as one of *Library Journal*'s "Movers and Shakers" for 2010. She earned her MLS from Kent State and was awarded her MCIW (Master Certified Internet Webmaster) in 2004. Visit her blog at www.meanlaura.com.

Printed in the United States of America
17 16 15 14 13   5 4 3 2 1

Extensive effort has gone into ensuring the reliability of the information in this book; however, the publisher makes no warranty, express or implied, with respect to the material contained herein.

ISBNs: 978-0-8389-1160-0 (paper); 978-0-8389-9631-7 (PDF): 978-0-8389-9632-4 (ePub); 978-0-8389-9633-1 (Kindle). For more information on digital formats, visit the ALA Store at alastore.ala.org and select eEditions.

Library of Congress Cataloging-in-Publication Data
Solomon, Laura, 1967-
  The librarian's nitty-gritty guide to social media / Laura Solomon.
    pages cm
  Includes bibliographical references and index.
  ISBN 978-0-8389-1160-0
  1. Online social networks—Library applications. 2. Social media. I. Title.
  Z674.75.S63S655 2013
  006.7'54—dc23
                                                                    2012027302

Book design in Palatino Linotype, Avenir, and Melbourne by Casey Bayer.
Cover illustration ©Marish/Shutterstock, Inc.
Interior cartoon illustrations by Diane Q. Klann.

♾ This paper meets the requirements of ANSI/NISO Z39.48-1992 (Permanence of Paper).

CONTENTS

INTRODUCTION

Social media is like teen sex. Everyone wants to do it. Nobody knows how. When it's finally done there's surprise it's not better.

—AVINASH KAUSHIK, ANALYTICS EVANGELIST

PROOF OF CONCEPT

On June 19, 2009, at approximately 4 p.m., the world changed for public libraries in Ohio. The Ohio governor made an unanticipated announcement, proposing a 50 percent cut to funding for public libraries. Previous to the announcement, Ohio was known as having some of the best public libraries in the nation. Considering that the vast majority of public libraries in the state received a good amount of their operating budgets from the state, this proposal would have decimated, or even closed, many of Ohio's libraries.

If the future existence of your institution is in doubt, what do you do? You do what library supporters in Ohio did: you mobilize. Many libraries mobilized their patrons, using their existing patron databases to send urgent e-mails asking them to call their legislators. Some libraries set up dedicated computers where patrons could send messages directly to the governor and the local representative. Others posted signs on their doors, stating their library would be permanently closed if the funding cut went through. These methods were invaluable in getting the word out.

Still other supporters turned to social media, which had the potential of reaching Ohio residents who were not active patrons of their local libraries.

These channels moved a great deal faster than almost any traditional form of communication and helped to mobilize tens of thousands of people who might otherwise not have been aware of the crisis.

Within an hour of the governor's announcement, the story was on Twitter. I created a Twitter hashtag (a way to categorize Twitter messages), #saveohiolibraries. The conversation collated around the hashtag, and it became one of the top forty most popular topics on Twitter. A Facebook group, Save Ohio Libraries, was started. It had over 50,000 members in less than three weeks. Mandy Knapp, a librarian from Worthington Libraries, began a website at www.saveohiolibraries.com, where she tracked the latest developments on the issue and where people could leave their own stories of why they needed their library. (And there were many stories!) Some patrons even put videos in support of libraries on YouTube. The social media movement was strong enough to garner support from such notables as author Neil Gaiman and celebrity blogger Perez Hilton. The Ohio library funding crisis had hit the national stage.

Between social media and other efforts put forth by libraries and their supporters, the Save Ohio Libraries movement made a huge impact at the State Capitol. Thousands of phone calls were made by patrons on their libraries' behalf, forcing state officials to add additional staff to handle them. Most legislators received between 37,000 and 45,000 e-mails in a one-week period, resulting in such a volume that an automatic response was put on the servers to try and keep the electronic traffic moving. Legislators commented to Lynda Murray, the director of government and legal services for the Ohio Library Council, that they had never seen anything like it at the Capitol.[1]

Although it was not possible to save all of the funds for Ohio's public libraries from the chopping block, a huge reduction in cutbacks was made; more than $147 million in state funding was saved, preventing the complete devastation of Ohio's nationally known libraries. As of this writing, despite the outpouring of support from Ohio's residents, many libraries are still struggling with the financial cuts. But things would have been much worse if the governor's proposal had come to full fruition.

IT'S NOT THE TOOL, IT'S THE WIELDER

Without social media, the reach of the campaign would have been more limited and much less effective. However, what many fail to understand is that social media doesn't just "happen." In our case, the social media efforts were primarily managed by a few people who were already very active in social networks and knew how to optimize their presence. These people understood core principles that make using these networks worth the work. Without these individuals, it's very likely that Save Ohio Libraries would not have had the impact in these online communities that it did. Many librarians and libraries simply did not have a presence in social media, or at least one that was influential enough to have any effect.

Many libraries do not understand that using social media successfully takes more than just having an account. Social media is a lot like the strategy game Othello: it's incredibly easy to learn but can take a long time to master. However, the minute-to-minute pace of social media does not allow for a long learning curve before claiming mastery. Many libraries take this to mean they should jump into the roaring river of online interaction, but by doing so they miss key concepts of how best to utilize the incredible tool at their fingertips. They waste time, resources, and opportunities to connect with the very people they want and need to reach.

Unlike traditional media, social media has few barriers. It's no longer a question of budget or acquiring the necessary tools; the vast majority of social media applications are free, and participating in social media is far easier than trying to produce a television commercial or print advertisement. The real need is for experienced social media staff in an arena where many mistakenly assume that having the tool is equivalent to having the expertise.

This book is my attempt not only to answer common questions libraries have about using social media but also to explain and demonstrate how libraries can be doing social media more effectively. There are many ways for libraries to enter the social media space, and there are pitfalls along the way; I know, I've seen almost all of them.

It's time to step up to your computer and learn how to do social media so it *matters*.

NOTE

1. Lynda Murray, e-mail message to author, January 8, 2010.

GETTING A (BETTER) GRIP ON SOCIAL MEDIA

The world, as it was, no longer is.

—ERIK QUALMAN, AUTHOR OF *SOCIALNOMICS*

THE TOOLS ARE EPHEMERAL

When it comes to discussing anything online, it's hard to argue with the fact that change is constant. How often have you or your coworkers complained that keeping up with everything new on the Web is nearly impossible? There's no doubt that the frenetic pace of online innovations can be daunting. Nevertheless, the pace is not likely to slow. Websites come and go as fast as the social media tools that empower them.

It's not hard to understand that *all* of the current social media tools are, at best, ephemeral. Accepting this idea of constant and immediate change may be hard for libraries, which historically act to preserve information. At the time of this writing, the popularity of MySpace has long been in serious decline, Facebook is considered the standard for social networks, and Google has introduced its own, Google+. What's popular today may be irrelevant tomorrow. Twitter may be replaced by something completely different a year from now. In order to be successful in online communities, libraries need to accept this fast pace of change and begin to move with it.

Unfortunately, some shortsighted individuals misconstrue the changing nature of online tools to mean that social media is a fad or something that libraries should avoid entirely. One of the most common questions I hear is, How do I convince my director that social media is important? To help answer that, I'll be introducing some methods to make your efforts more effective.

BOTTOM LINE ▶ Social media sites will change. Concepts will not. Be flexible.

UNDERSTANDING THE LIBRARY'S PLACE IN SOCIAL MEDIA

Librarians may know about the various social media tools and may even teach their patrons how to use them. They may also have some vague idea about using them to promote programs or collections. Most, however, are truly stymied when it comes to understanding how best to use these tools to their benefit. Even more critically, they may fail to understand basic social media concepts, such as how to build trust and reciprocity (social capital), resulting in the library being effectively irrelevant in a particular online community.

It's easy to get a free account on any of the hundreds of social media sites that currently exist, but social media is not about coverage or even necessarily about numbers. It's about making *connections*. That might seem like a touchy-feely way to gauge its value, especially if you're an administrator, but part of learning to handle social media interaction appropriately is to understand that numbers are not the primary consideration. It's true that metrics are something that should be tracked as part of a library's social media work, but social media's goals are quite different from those of traditional advertising media. In fact, I would argue that social media isn't particularly effective for pure advertising. So why participate in a social media community at all?

Simply using the tools to proclaim, "Come to our library's cool program!" won't fly online. Social media is not a one-way broadcast; it can act as a unique bridge that has never been available to libraries before. Social media can do something no other medium can: directly engage and connect our patrons—to the library and to each other. Knowing how to use Facebook, Twitter, MySpace, or the next "it" social media site is just the beginning. Effective social media takes some thought, a lot of time, and, yes, some careful planning. Until you unlock the potential of online social media, it might seem that it is just a stream of consciousness of the masses and, as a communication method, largely pointless.

Librarians often envision the role of the library as a community center. Social media allows them to put this philosophy directly into practice. Think carefully about what the word *community* connotes: a place where various people communicate and interact with one another. If a library uses social media only as a broadcast medium to get the word out, it is not participating in a community but rather using a version of a bullhorn to promote itself to a crowd.

When a library involves itself in social media, it first and foremost has to understand that it's going to be expected to *interact.* To do otherwise is to fail. Let me say that again: To do otherwise is to fail. By failing to participate in conversations and relationships, the library is essentially declaring that it will simply maintain its traditional role as a depository of knowledge.

Libraries are for the people and of the people, to borrow a phrase. Social media is no different. In other words, even though a library is an organizational entity, once it enters the social realm it is perceived as a *person* and will need to act and speak accordingly.

BOTTOM LINE   Interact with people in social media, or risk becoming irrelevant.

LETTING GO OF THE MESSAGE

The successful use of social media requires companies and organizations to "let go of the message." This means that there has to be an inherent understanding on the part of the institution that the staff in charge of public relations no longer has control over what is said about the organization. In many cases, an organization's social networks may act as an informal PR department. For better or for worse, many conversations are happening about businesses (and libraries) online, and these interchanges are not controlled by any "official" entity.

Library administrators have to understand that *patrons* now control the message. This can be even harder yet to comprehend in the context of social media. There is no longer a one-to-many broadcast model for a message. Now, each person participating in a social media site's service constitutes a node on a network that serves many-to-many communication. There is no "official" voice or moderator. Theoretically, all participants have equal standing in these communities, regardless of what positions they might hold in the offline world. This means that people who *don't* work for your library have as much (some might say more) say as people who *do* as to what gets said about it.

There is also a tendency for administrators to think only of what they perceive to be worst-case scenarios: What happens if someone makes a negative comment? What happens if the library gets a bad review? The fact is, people have always had not-so-flattering things to say about libraries. The channels for *hearing* those comments, however, were not so wide open or publicly accessible as they now are. This is our twenty-first-century reality: Conversations have moved to the online realm and have, therefore, broadened the scope of their audiences. It's likely that the possible size of the audience and the speed at which news can travel via social media are what makes many library administrators nervous about embracing it.

Although it's possible that negative commentary will have repeated airings, it's crucial to remember that, under most circumstances, the number of positive remarks will almost always outweigh the negative ones. People want to take ownership of the library's "brand" and want to be able to brag about it, just as they likely do with organizations they are a part of or products or performers they admire.

Bluntly speaking, there is no practical way to control what is or is not said about a library. Libraries that choose to participate in social networks have to internalize this truth. Patrons are no longer just at the receiving end of communications. Patrons now receive *and* send. Some will inevitably say something the library won't agree with; this is the nature of conversation after all. Just keep in mind that social media involvement allows the library to build one-to-one relationships with patrons that can result in more loyalty and possibly advocacy later on.

BOTTOM LINE ▸ Giving up control is hard, but the worst case scenario rarely happens. Even if it does, it is far outweighed by the potential reach a library can have via social media.

GETTING ADMINISTRATIVE BUY-IN

Social media might be old hat to you. Maybe you already participate in a social networking site and want to know how to maximize your time in these conversations. Or, perhaps you're in the all-too-common position of having to convince a library administrator that social media is not a fad or a waste of time. In libraries, knowing how to do social media well isn't enough; you also need a social media foundation that is determined by two factors:

- Media-competent staff who are actually in charge of the social media presence of the library
- Level of support from the library's administration for social media

It can be an unfortunate reality for library staff who may have the media expertise but not the backing of library administrators. Social media efforts will likely end in failure without a director's buy-in. At some point, no matter how adept you might be at navigating the social media terrain, you are going to need backup. How will your administration expect you to handle negative comments? How does the director want questions answered that come in via social networks? At the very least, you will need to invest time in building social capital. How much time will your director support?

The first step, of course, is to show that social media has a direct benefit for your library. Administrators can often be industry-insular; in other words, if the staff cannot point directly to another library where a social media endeavor has already been a success, administrators may be reluctant to consider anything else as legitimate. Also, much of the library profession tends to be traditional in its approach, and administrators can be inherently reluctant to examine strategies from other types of organizations. This can be very self-limiting and rarely leads to real innovation or change.

I am often asked for specific examples of libraries using social media well, and I can seldom cite any. More often, I point to other types of nonprofits or even large corporations

"So you see, I need to spend six hours in the staff workroom developing relationships with patrons." *(Caption by Melissa Percic)*

that "get it." "Getting it" doesn't mean jumping on the Web 2.0 bandwagon. What it does mean is that these organizations or companies understand that online communication has moved beyond just transmitting a message to a largely receptive audience. Successful social media means that the organization is ready to have two-way conversations online, even if they are negative or uncomfortable. The organization understands that it is involved in building a long-term relationship, not just in completing a quick, anonymous transaction. Companies such as Dell and Zappos.com are famous for their customer relations via social media channels, primarily because they engage directly and consistently with their customers online and under public scrutiny.

Not every social media tool is for every person or every library; some libraries may not even have a demographic that uses this type of communication yet. However, for those libraries that are aware their patrons are out there on social networks, it's critical that they also understand how social media will enhance the library experience. Those patrons have expectations for the members of their online communities. These patrons want their social media connections to act like real people, talk like real people, and not always put themselves first. If your library's director will not allow you to act in accordance with those expectations, it's likely that your future efforts will be rejected.

SO WHAT CAN YOU DO?

How do you convince the reluctant director? There's no magic wand here, but the following sections present some avenues to explore.

Education

An education campaign has to be part of your exertions; facts are important.

Put Information in Front of Them

Find brief, entertaining articles or blog posts that not only explain social media but also showcase examples of how social media provided a concrete benefit. Print them out and send them to the director with a sticky note: "Hi, thought you would find this interesting." Printing something out shows more effort on your part and is less likely to be totally ignored than an e-mail. The sticky note gives it a more personal touch, too. Be sure to tell them you'll follow up so they know you expect them to glance at it.

Tell Stories

I find myself telling personal stories when I'm explaining social media. Anecdotes provide a human perspective and make interesting hooks for people new to the concepts. (After all, social media is all about people.) I often tell the story of how I was introduced to Twitter. At first, I honestly thought it was the dumbest online tool I'd ever seen. Once I saw it in use as a way to have informative conversations during conference sessions (a conference back channel), a lightbulb went on and now I can't live without it. I also tell stories about how other aspects of my life have been affected by social media. My husband and I reconnected with the best man from our wedding because someone I met at a conference started following me on Twitter. I have a friend who met his wife via a virtual world. This kind of thing happens all the time. Social media is making the world smaller, and people are connecting to one another in new ways. Show the personal impact of social media to bring your point home.

Highlight the Facts to Diminish the Fears

Does your administrator believe no one will want to interact with a library? A study published by eMarketer in 2009, "Social Network Marketing Expands Sphere," showed that more than half of the users of social networks have followed or become a fan of a brand online.[1] If someone is going to become a fan of local restaurants on Facebook, they may also want to be a fan of their library. Is the director afraid that people will say negative things? The same study found that users are much more likely to rave than to rant. For nearly every concern, there are facts, figures, and case studies to address it. Check the bibliography for some resources to help you.

Downplay the Technology

This is not about any cool technologies or your enthusiasm for them. Your director is looking at the big picture. Ultimately, it will come down to whether or not social media is good for the library. Technology becomes less relevant than what the library will potentially get out of it: more potential support at levy time and advocates who will call their representative when funding comes under fire. These deliverables may mean more to an administrator than the technology.

Explain What Happens If an Outsider Hijacks the Library's Name

The practice of taking someone/something else's name online is called *brandjacking,* and even if your library isn't in social media space, someone could grab its name. If that were to happen, it would be incredibly difficult to shut down the culprit. Meanwhile, there's no knowing what damage might have been done to the library's reputation. Claiming an identity on social networks is just as important as buying domain names for your library. Even if your director isn't eager to start posting status updates, the library should at least go through the steps of claiming the library's name by setting up accounts on popular networks. Once your library is there, it will likely start accumulating followers. At that point, you can emphasize to your administration that these fans are expecting some communication.

Keeping Up with the "Competition"

If your director is a very competitive person, chances are good he or she will want to investigate what other libraries are doing. Find libraries in your region or state that are already engaged in social media. Specifically, make an effort to find examples where the library is interacting directly with patrons and not just broadcasting promotions such as program announcements. Look for the libraries that are actually engaging in conversations in a public online forum with their patrons. These libraries are your library's role models. Send links or printouts to members of your administration with a brief note: "Look at what Example Library is doing. They're talking directly with their patrons online!" Your competitive director will likely be intrigued to find out more.

Show What's Already Out There

Search Google and all of the major social networks for your library's name. Check Yelp for reviews about your library, and location-based services such as Foursquare to see if anyone has posted any tips about your branches. Collate whatever you find and send it to the director. If your search is especially fruitful, you'll also turn up some not-so-flattering things as well as positive or neutral ones. Why is this kind of feedback a good thing? Because it clearly shows you can't effectively respond unless you're in the space with the person who posted it. If you don't find any negative items, it still is clear proof that people *are* talking about the library in social media spaces. The library needs to be in that social media space to listen and connect.

Recommend Something Else

If you've been pushing Twitter without results, consider moving to a push for Facebook. It could be the director has specific objections to a particular tool rather than to social media as a whole.

Hand-Holding

In some cases, the administrator you are seeking to convince may be interested but not sure where to start. Being overwhelmed with all of the choices is not uncommon. Try to remember what it was like when you were a complete novice and what you wished someone had done for you then.

Invite Them to Get Involved

Granted, it might be a bit awkward to "friend" your director on Facebook. But what about something like Twitter? Or LinkedIn? Most social media sites provide members with ways to invite nonmembers to join. Remember, it's a lot like a party—it's easier to go there if you already know someone. Again, follow-up is crucial to success. If your director doesn't respond right away, be sure to ask if he or she received the invitation.

Sit Down and Offer to Help

Sometimes, you just need to *be* there. Offer to spend an hour walking the director through the social network of choice and help in finding colleagues to connect with that you both already know. Show how to add apps (specialized computer program applications) to Facebook or LinkedIn accounts. Just be sure not to present too much information too fast.

Do Something Specific to Your Library

Sometimes, the best way to get buy-in is to show that using a social media tool will do something very specific. Look for something that will interest your library's administration, such as creating video tutorials for using the online catalog or getting feedback on a new service. But beware the "when you have a hammer, every problem looks like a nail" approach; don't let your enthusiasm for social media become a solution in search of a problem.

In-House Training

When I was in school, I always enjoyed the opportunities to go beyond the typical take-a-test/write-a-report assignment model. If you're training library staff, ask them to show what they learned by writing a blog post or making a quick video, or even by creating a photo slideshow that's posted to a site like Flickr or Picasa. Give them latitude to do something creative that also makes use of online tools and that they can share with the rest of the staff.

Conferences

No library can afford to send everyone to every conference. Introduce your director (and any attending staff) to Twitter hashtags (words or phrases preceded by the symbol #). The staff going to the conference can send tweets with relevant points, marked with the hashtag for the conference (for example, #nameofconference); the director and other interested staff can follow them and other conference-goers on Twitter. By following the hashtag, people from your library will get a nearly real-time sense of what's happening at the conference, and more important, they'll also connect in a new way with their coworkers.

Promote New Initiatives

Is your library about to do something new on a large scale? Self-check machines? Print management? New ILS? Whatever it is, an internal blog to track announcements, information, and feedback may be perfect for introducing new social media tools. It may also reduce the need for formal training time down the road. Not every blog needs to be forever; some have a limited lifespan or purpose. A blog (with comments turned on!) is a good way to experiment internally with some of the "feel" of social media. You could also open up the blog and comments to the public at large and get patron feedback on the new service.

BOTTOM LINE ▶ Everyone has an "Aha!" moment when experimenting with new social media. I did with Twitter. It may be your director's aha is yet to come. Keep sending relevant search results and articles. Hang in there and be an advocate for social media, but be aware that people may be turned off if you become too zealous. Keep the enthusiasm but focus on facts. Getting buy-in from your library's administration may be challenging at first. Chip away at resistance, try different methods, but don't give up.

Getting Staff Buy-in

You may think you're ready to begin once you've been given the green light from your library's administrator. You'd be at least partially correct; getting administrative approval *is* absolutely essential. However, getting buy-in doesn't end with your library's director. Although it is possible to run a successful social media campaign without the approval of one's colleagues, it is considerably more difficult.

Coworkers who don't understand social media or the library's reason for wanting to engage in it can not only make your job harder but also damage your efforts. Library staff with negative attitudes can undermine you by refusing to provide needed content, creating delays, spreading rumors or gossip, or ignoring the library's social media policy. These staff become obstacles that you have to work around rather than sources of support.

How do you bring these staff members on board with the library's social media ventures? Fortunately, all of the methods you may have used with your library's director are just as applicable to other staff. Some of the methods described in the previous section may work better than others, depending on the person you're working with. Just as with your administrator, you may need to try different approaches to get the support you need. Following are some additional things to consider when getting backing from your colleagues.

One Size Does Not Fit All

Consider each staff person separately. It's unlikely that one person's objections to social media involvement are identical to someone else's. Find out what each individual cares about and address your efforts to those aspects. Are they worried that it will somehow add to their workload? Do they not understand the usefulness of Twitter or think that Facebook is still only for college students? Getting buy-in means proving to reluctant staff that social media is not only relevant to the library's needs but also to their individual needs and concerns. Make sure you have the data or policies readily available to back you up.

Never Assume Everyone Knows What You Are Talking About

Many people who are resistant to social media may only have *heard* of some of the social media sites like Facebook or Twitter and may not have actually used them. Or, if they have tried them, they may have only used a site briefly and not understood that the benefits come after long-term participation. Don't assume that everyone is on a social site like Facebook and understands terms such as *friending, apps,* or *wall.* By explaining site-specific terms and customs, you increase the chances of selling the benefits to staff.

Training Can Make a Significant Difference

In addition to educating staff individually, group training can help break down resistance. One of the most successful projects for doing this has been the 23 Things project, originally created by Helene Blowers and launched with the staff of the Public Library of Charlotte and Mecklenburg County in

North Carolina.[2] The 23 Things project is a discovery-learning program that helps staff become comfortable with social media technologies by asking them to try different online tools. It has become very popular in the United States and internationally as a way to train staff in the basics of using social media. Hands-on experience can bridge many gaps in understanding.

Ensure That Staff Has Time to Learn before Social Media Is Rolled Out to the Public

Just as with any new initiative or resource at your library, your staff members will feel more secure if they see it in action before their patrons do. Even if they are not the ones doing the posting, seeing social media in action (as with the 23 Things program) can increase their comfort level with how social media works.

BOTTOM LINE ▶   Staff buy-in isn't as critical as administrative buy-in, but not having it can make a social media coordinator's job a lot harder. Make a serious effort to educate and alleviate fears with information and hands-on training.

DON'T SABOTAGE YOUR EFFORTS

Many people, when attempting to convince administrators or staff, make a common mistake that can undermine or totally derail their efforts. An overly eager staff may come across as evangelizing to administrators and other colleagues, rather than providing meaningful examples or data about social media. If you take this route, you risk sounding more like a zealous teenager than a professional trying to convince an administrator to change what is essentially the library's communication model.

Administrators also need to be able to rationalize the costs involved. It's very easy to say that social media is free; after all, virtually no social network charges for an account, and it's just the staff time involved, right? Unfortunately, if your library wants to do social media well, there are real costs to doing social media right. As you'll learn from reading this book, just using social media to blast a message is counterproductive. Real social media takes a considerable amount of time, which may be more than you or your director initially expected. You will also spend time and money creating related elements, such as social media policies and graphics for social media avatars and pages. Effective social networking also requires support in other media:

Will your library need to reprint business cards or signage to reflect its presence on various online networks? What about integrating social media into the library's website? How much time or money will that require? When you are working to achieve administrative support of social media, you should be able to give a clear picture of the real costs weighed against the real benefits of your library's participation.

Your ebullient support of social media should not be the only foundation upon which you build a business case. Even if the director you are trying to sell is a social media fanatic, you need to remember that he or she may in turn need to justify this venture to a library board, the library's patrons, and possibly even local journalists or media. Case studies, articles, and actual examples of libraries doing social media to good effect are your best strategies. To be successful with your case, you need to provide colleagues and administrators with the tools that *they* can use with others.

BOTTOM LINE ▶   Don't let your enthusiasm overwhelm your need to present a solid argument for social media in your library.

IS SOCIAL MEDIA RIGHT FOR YOUR LIBRARY?

After reading this far, you may be wondering if your library has what it takes to do social media. Perhaps it's lacking administrative support or enough staff time to do it well. It may be that your library serves a small or rural population, making it seem unlikely that social media will have any measurable impact. The question that I get frequently from library staff about social media is, "We already have so much to do. Do we really *need* to do this, too?"

If one only looks at the number of abandoned library blogs, Twitter accounts, and Facebook Pages, it becomes clear that a lot of libraries, at least initially, jumped on the bandwagon. Many of these libraries believed the hype about easy marketing through social media. Undoubtedly, they also fell victim to the realities of social media work: the time, the costs, and the difficulties of engaging patrons consistently. Nearly all of these failures can be attributed to a lack of planning, as well as a lack of understanding about what effective social media work entails.

As mentioned earlier, evangelizing about social media doesn't help build a case for what is going to be a long-term effort. It's less important to be enthusiastic than it is to be realistic. It doesn't matter if social media works for hundreds of other libraries if, in the end, it won't work for yours. While many well-known library speakers and bloggers may loudly cheer the benefits of social media, it's crucial to figure out if those benefits are a good fit for *your* library. Even if they are, how much work will it take to achieve the result you want, and is your library prepared to invest what is required?

Social media's strength and influence in our world continues to grow. However, does this mean that your library will wither away from not having a Facebook Page? Extremely unlikely. In the future, having a social media presence may become mission-critical. For now, if your library can't envision any real return on investment (ROI), it's all right to give social media a pass. For the moment, I think it's untruthful to claim that social media is right for every organization. However, remember that it is important for your library to keep an ear to the ground and at least monitor its online reputation (see chapter 8). Additionally, the importance of social media *is* increasing. There may come a point at which not having a social media presence is much the same as not having a website was a decade ago.

BOTTOM LINE Social media isn't for every library, not at this point. However, no library should look to escape it completely or forever. Social media is changing the world, make no mistake. If your library can't or shouldn't do it now, it should be planning for future social media endeavors.

NOTES

1. eMarketer, "Social Network Marketing Expands Sphere," August 31, 2009, www .emarketer.com/Article.aspx?R=1007252.
2. Helene Blowers, "Learning 2.0," May 2, 2006, http://plcmcl2-about.blogspot.com.

GETTING STARTED

Instead of researching the best ways to engage, many
businesses create accounts across multiple social
networks and publish content without a plan or purpose.
However, businesses that conduct research will find
a rewarding array of options and opportunities.

—BRIAN SOLIS, AUTHOR OF *ENGAGE!*

GOALS FIRST: WHAT DOES SUCCESS LOOK LIKE?

Setting goals is a step that many libraries choose to skip over, believing that
their mere presence on a social network is the only goal. Do not, repeat, *do not*
allow your library to enter social media without knowing what it wants to get
out of it! If there is no clear picture of what "success" looks like, your library
isn't ready to enter these communities. It's essential to figure out what your
library wants from its efforts and how it plans to achieve a successful outcome.

What might goals for a library social media program look like? After all,
when there isn't a specific product to sell, how can you measure success? It
doesn't have to be very complicated. Some examples might be the following:

- More people at events and programs
- Better overall awareness of the library
- More blog subscribers
- New knowledge about your patrons and how they view the library
- More "buzz" about the library

Focus on just a few goals, no more than three to begin with. Keep these at the forefront of all of your library's social media work. Whenever your library posts a status update or uploads some kind of media, look at the list of goals and see which one it's contributing to. If the answer is none, reframe it or drop it and do something that will better serve the library's objectives.

If one of your library's goals is engaging with patrons, then make sure that you're always trying to answer the question, Will this post/update/item cause more patrons to start a conversation with the library? Chances are, if your library is simply promoting a program, it's unlikely to elicit any real response. Efforts to engage patrons may require creativity and planning to be effective.

The next step is to figure out how you're actually going to measure your goals. For instance, will you quantify buzz as a certain number of blog comments or Facebook wall posts? Can you quantify awareness with a particular number of retweets on Twitter? If you can't find a way to measure whether or not you're meeting the goal, then the goal is likely not a good one or needs to be refocused. As with any new undertaking, it's important to know how to benchmark results in order to evaluate the undertaking as a whole. Otherwise, you won't know if your efforts are worthwhile in the long run.

BOTTOM LINE ▶ Figuring out your library's social media goals doesn't have to be terribly complex, but it does have to be the first step.

CHOOSING SOCIAL MEDIA SITES

A question I am often asked is, What social media should my library spend time on? There are, of course, pros and cons to each site, and new networks are appearing all the time. It certainly makes the most sense to invest time in only those that are popular and have critical mass. But how do you know which ones? Libraries are often short of both time and staff and need to be able to focus their efforts where they will really count.

In the case of a business, a social media strategist would begin by investigating which social networks most closely match the target demographic for that business. This can be more difficult to do in the case of a library, which draws patrons from many different demographic profiles. Since the likely goal is to reach as many people as possible with the least amount of effort, it makes sense for a library to pick those sites that are most popular. Beyond popularity, the library needs to be able to support the type of content featured on a particular social site. For instance, if a library isn't planning to release new, original videos regularly, YouTube will not be a good choice.

Keep the library's objectives in mind as well. Assuming that at least one of the library's goals is to converse directly with patrons, make sure that the site supports ways to send messages and share links.

Lastly, conduct some in-house market research. Poll your patrons! You may be surprised to find most are on MySpace rather than on Facebook, or vice versa. You may find that many people in your area might have moved to Google+, believing it to have feature or privacy advantages over Facebook. It's never ideal to guess at what your patrons want. Instead, begin your library's immersion in social interaction in the offline world by asking people what social media they participate in. This is also a good way to gather a core interest group to which you can promote your new social media presence.

BOTTOM LINE ▶ There is no single "right" social media service that will fit every library. Spend time doing research with patrons and know what kind of content your library can consistently support.

COMPARING SOCIAL MEDIA SITES

When you start doing your research, it's important to know what kind of social media your library is interested in. A blog is not the same as a social networking site, which is a very broad-based social tool. Social networking sites also are not the same as microblogging sites (e.g., Twitter, where posts are extremely short and functionality is much more limited).

As pointed out previously, social media sites are being created or upgraded constantly. A good way to find feature comparisons of the most popular sites of the moment is to search online. Side-by-side comparison charts are easy to find via your favorite search engine, but be very sure that you are using the correct terminology in your searches. For example, searching for "social networking sites comparison" may not bring up microblogging tools such as Twitter or Pheed; in other words, be sure you're doing "apples to apples" comparisons.

There are hundreds of sites in this genre, so make sure that your initial research includes obtaining the most recent metrics possible. As of this writing, some major social media websites have hit mainstream use. Some of these may be better suited for your library's needs than others. Table 2.1 gives you some basic demographics for the social media sites that libraries are the most likely to use.

TABLE 2.1 **Demographics for top social media sites used by libraries**

	Percentage male in 2011	Percentage female in 2011	Average age in 2011
Facebook	51%	49%	38
Google+	70%	30%	Most popular with ages 25–34 (no average yet available)
Twitter	45%	55%	39
MySpace	36%	64%	32

If your library's decision is going to be based primarily on numbers, there's no question that Facebook is at the top of the heap. Not only does it have the highest number of active users, but more than 50 percent of those users log in to their Facebook accounts every day and more than 1.5 million businesses have pages on the site.[1] No matter the size of your library, if it can choose only one place to have a social media presence, Facebook is almost certainly the best bet across most demographics.

As widespread as Facebook use is, however, it may not be the only place your library should be. Once again, you'll need to go back to your original goals. Not every social media tool will be a good fit for your objectives. For example, if you are using social media primarily to spread the word about an upcoming tax levy, MySpace is probably not a good choice. Not only is the average age of MySpace users younger (meaning that a good part of the demographic is not even old enough to vote), but also your library's content is not a good match for the kinds of content that these users want. On the other hand, if you are looking mostly to have a presence that may create more conversations with teens, MySpace may be the way to go (although more current metrics indicate both Twitter and Tumblr are better options for connecting with teens). If your library is promoting an event that will draw mostly women, pushing it hard on Google+, which is primarily male, will unlikely get many attendees. Figures 2.1–2.3 summarize the kinds of content that users seek on Facebook, MySpace, and Twitter. Note that Twitter is a significantly better tool for spreading breaking news than either Facebook or

MySpace. If your library needs to get a message out urgently, Twitter is the best pick by far. This is a reason why libraries should, whenever possible, maintain at least a Twitter *and* a Facebook account. They are different tools with different strengths.

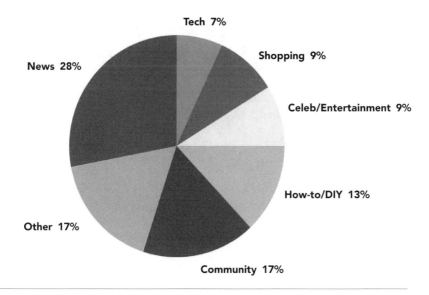

FIGURE 2.1 **Facebook content breakdown**

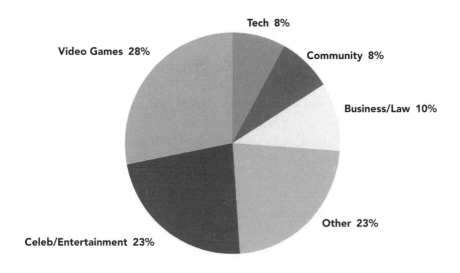

FIGURE 2.2 **MySpace content breakdown**

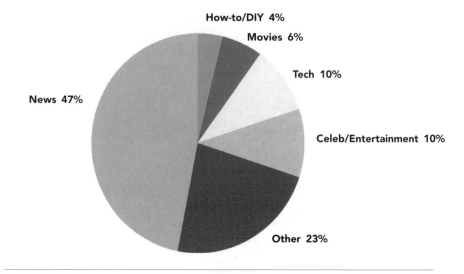

FIGURE 2.3 **Twitter content breakdown**

BOTTOM LINE ▶ If your library can be in only one place online, Facebook should be it. Ideally, however, your library should maintain an active presence at least on Facebook and on Twitter. They are very different social instruments with different strengths. Find the best fit for your library based on the demographics you are trying to reach and your library's goals.

WRITING A SOCIAL MEDIA POLICY FOR YOUR STAFF

Many social media experts clearly state that every organization should have a social media policy. The very public nature of social media services may bring potential hazards that you should anticipate and address. Stories abound of awkward incidents involving social media and oversharing or hotheaded comments. (There's even a website devoted to embarrassing Facebook threads, www.failbooking.com.)

It's unrealistic (and counterproductive) to ban a library's employees from using social media or mentioning their workplace online. A better approach is to plainly spell out guidelines that employees should keep in mind. A social media policy can go a long way toward preventing PR fiascoes.

Ellyssa Kroski, writing for *School Library Journal*, laid out several criteria that should be included in such a policy.[2] The most important of these are as follows:

- *Include a disclaimer.* Include a statement on blogs and social sites in which the employee points out that his or her statements are not those of his or her employer, the library.
- *Don't share confidential information.* This includes information about coworkers or patrons or information that is sensitive in nature.
- *Use good judgment.* Employees should always consider the image they might be portraying of the library. Everything an employee posts will be archived by search engines, permanently. Remember the newspaper test: If the post wouldn't survive scrutiny in a newspaper or some other vehicle of mass media distribution, it's not appropriate. If in doubt, consult the employee manual or a supervisor.
- *Respect copyright law and accuracy.* Employees should give credit when they quote others, regardless of which social media site they may be using. A direct link to the quoted material is the preferable convention. If something later turns out to be inaccurate, the employee needs to take full responsibility and post a retraction or correction. It's far better to admit a mistake quickly than to attempt to camouflage or ignore it.

A social media policy doesn't have to be a long, wordy document. The point is not to cover every possible contingency or make using social media so intimidating for the library's employees that they won't want to engage in it. Rather, the idea is to show that the library actually supports employees' efforts and acknowledges social media as something that staff very likely want to participate in. Providing written guidelines gives these employees a strong foundation on which to stand.

Two excellent examples of library social media policies are the following:

- University of Texas Southwestern Medical Center Library (http://units.sla.org/chapter/ctx/UTSouthwesternLibrarySocialMediaPolicy_LLT_Final.pdf)
- Whitman Public Library (http://aklaconference2011.pbworks.com/f/whitmanPL-socialmedia.pdf)

If you'd like to examine social media policies from other nonprofits, government agencies, and various kinds of businesses, try the Social Media Governance Policy Database (http://socialmediagovernance.com/policies.php), which is fully searchable and has more than 120 examples.

SOCIAL NETWORKING

Board Policy:

DATE APPROVED: 06/18/2009
EFFECTIVE DATE: 07/01/2009
REPLACING POLICY EFFECTIVE: 00/00/0000

The Library recognizes the value in the exchange of ideas and information through the various online community and communication opportunities available to its employees. The Library expects its employees to utilize online social networking communities in a manner that is consistent with the procedural paragraphs below.

Administrative Procedures:

DATE APPROVED: 06/04/2009
EFFECTIVE DATE: 07/01/2009
REPLACING PROCEDURE EFFECTIVE: 00/00/0000

A. Common sense should be applied by employees in that this policy cannot prescribe acceptable and unacceptable speech. Employees should have no expectation that what is said or written in an online community social network or blog will be protected by the same levels of privacy typically associated with a conversation.

B. Statements that may be construed as threatening, harassing or defamatory in the non-social networking environment are equally restricted in the online social networking environment. They will be subject to review and consideration under all other applicable Library policies and existing laws, and based on content and severity, may be addressed through provisions of the corrective counseling process.

C. Personal blogs should have clear disclaimers that the views expressed by the author in the blog are the author's alone and do not represent the views of the Library. Be clear and write in first person.

D. Employees should not represent their statements in an online social networking community as reflective of official Library policy or position. Nor should employees establish an online presence on sites such as Facebook or blog and represent it as the Library, or a Library-sponsored entity.

E. Under no circumstances should confidential Library strategies, personnel disciplinary situations, etc., be posted to an online community.

F. Information published on blog(s) should comply with the Library's confidentiality policy. This also applies to comments posted on other forums and social networking sites.

G. Do not reference or cite Library clients, partners, or customers without their express consent.

H. Respect copyright laws, and reference or cite sources appropriately.

FIGURE 2.4 **Columbus Metropolitan Library social media policy. Courtesy of the Columbus Metropolitan Library, Columbus, Ohio.**

I. Library logos and trademarks may not be used without written consent.

J. In the event that the Library sponsors a blog or social networking site, non-exempt employees are not required nor expected to participate on this site during non-working hours.

K. Other than for work-related assignments, non-exempt employees may access and utilize social networking sites while at work only during their approved lunch and work break periods.

L. Exempt employees are expected to limit their access and time spent on social networking sites during working hours to the period of time that is consistent with meeting the demands of their position.

M. Managers should address directly with the individual employee those situations where it appears the employee is engaged in excessive non-work-related online social networking activities.

Related Policies & Forms:
- Code of Conduct
- Confidentiality
- Harassment
- Official Statements on Behalf of the Library
- Use of Library Communications Technologies

The Columbus Metropolitan Library in Columbus, Ohio, has a very good policy that other libraries may want to use as a model (see figure 2.4). It's not overly long, yet covers the salient points.

BOTTOM LINE ▶ Effective social media involvement takes time and planning. Don't skip these steps.

NOTES

1. "Facebook Facts & Figures (history & statistics)," 2011, www.website-monitoring .com/blog/2011/10/14/facebook-facts-and-figures-2011-infographic.
2. Ellyssa Kroski, "Should Your Library Have a Social Media Policy?" *School Library Journal*, October 1, 2009, www.schoollibraryjournal.com/article/CA6699104.html.

UNDERSTANDING
SOCIAL CAPITAL

Those who ignore the party/conversation/network when they are content and decide to drop in when they need the network may not succeed. It's pretty easy to spot those that are just joining the network purely to take—not to give. Therefore, be part of the party/conversation/network before you need anything from anyone.

—JEREMIAH OWYANG, WEB-STRATEGIST.COM

During the Save Ohio Libraries movement in 2009, some libraries in Ohio jumped into Twitter. Undoubtedly, they saw Twitter as another avenue for getting the word out about the imminent and catastrophic budget cuts being proposed by Ohio's governor. However, there were two major factors preventing them from really using Twitter as an effective rallying tool:

- *Lack of followers.* Numbers are not the only criterion for social media success (and certainly not the most important one), but some followers are needed to spread a message. When an organization jumps into a social media tool during a crisis without followers developed over time, there is a distinct lack of audience to hear any pleas for help.
- *Lack of social capital.* Social capital is what allows any organization or individual to make requests of its followers successfully. Think of social capital like funds in a sort of intangible bank account that you add to by listening to, engaging with, and doing favors for others. Each time you make a request, you are drawing on that account. If

no social capital has been established from which to draw, actions requested of others are likely to be ignored.

Having social capital is, in many ways, equivalent to having credibility in a selected online community. It means that others recognize you as someone who provides value and promotes content from others in addition to your own. Social capital can only be earned over time by participating appropriately in the community.

EARNING SOCIAL CAPITAL

Gaining social capital really means becoming a strong, consistent member of the online community. People expect reciprocity, so it is important to remember that a good reputation offline does not necessarily translate into social capital online. Although your library may gain followers or friends based on reputation alone, they may or may not engage with or advocate for your library. Building a social media reputation means giving back.

"Please, pretty please, help the library???"
As a social media tactic, this is not effective.

How can your library go about earning the trust of its patrons online? There are several ways, and like all relationships, these methods require effort and time to develop. For most, a combination of the following actions will usually benefit a library's online reputation.

Thank Your Patrons

People like to be recognized for their contributions. When someone comments on your library blog, even if it's just to agree, thank him or her. If the commenter says something negative, express appreciation for the feedback. It shows that your library is listening to all points of view and values constructive input. If someone posts something about the library to their Facebook Page or retweets for your library on Twitter, acknowledge and thank that person. It's an easy way to engage your patrons and promote positive feelings toward the library.

Ask for Opinions

Nearly everyone likes to be asked for an opinion. Ask for readers' favorite Oprah Book Club pick or their favorite program at the library. Try asking for opinions on the worst book ever written! The more controversial the question, the more feedback it will likely get. Although generating controversy for its own sake may not be your library's goal, facilitating conversation between the library and others is something you want. Don't wait for someone to start a discussion; be proactive and initiate exchanges of ideas and opinions on a variety of topics that interest your patrons on an ongoing basis.

Offer Links to Other Sites of Interest

It's very common to pass along interesting links via social media channels; however, posting only links to your library's assets (e.g., catalog, programs, or website) is just another method of self-promotion and not a form of engagement. Have you seen a funny video on YouTube? Pass the link along. Do the same for interesting blog posts and articles. Just make sure they are not written by anyone on your library staff or you may diminish the open forum you are trying to encourage.

Retweet Your Followers

If your library is on Twitter, the person who is responsible for the Twitter account should learn the syntax of retweeting and do so whenever and as often as possible. Typically, a retweet starts with "RT @[Twitter handle of person being retweeted]." For example: "RT @laurasolomon I'm so glad my library allows me to reserve books online!" You can also add a brief commentary, such as "Yes we do! RT @laurasolomon I'm so glad my library allows me to reserve books online." If one of your library's followers says something that might be of interest to others, pass it along. Bear in mind that you may ask your followers to pass on something later to advocate for the library. Build up your social capital now, so that you can ask for favors later.

Always Give Credit

This applies to all content, not just retweets. Do you want to promote a new program that was a patron's idea? Name the patron and link directly to that person if you can. An old newspaper adage is that "names sell papers." The library may not be selling anything in the literal sense, but the concept holds. People want to be involved when they know their name is going to be promoted. This is another reason why photos of patrons at programs are a popular way to get people to visit a website; people invariably want to see themselves or someone they know. The library is an organization that cannot exist without its community, so be sure to acknowledge that community whenever and as often as possible.

Encourage Feedback

One way that many people commonly use social media is as an outlet for venting their frustrations. This is the perfect opportunity for your library to hone its social media "voice." Frustrated people often just want to be heard. If one of your library's friends or followers is venting, expressing empathy can help forge a relationship. It can also serve to show that your library is "human"—that real people who care work there. It also shows that the library is paying attention to its patrons, and its response can help them feel important and part of the community.

People like to have opportunities to talk about themselves. Ask people in your library's network about items they post or follow up on something they posted earlier. In addition to asking, tell them about interesting things that happen at the library. This isn't promoting a program—this is a more personal, less self-serving kind of making a status update. Maybe you received a unique or interesting reference question? Post it along with the answer. Pique people's interest in what you do and what makes the library tick.

Provide Information People Care About

Online, your library needs to provide value to its friends and followers. If there's information about something happening in your community, use your online channels to pass on that information. When promoting a library event, be sure your post answers the question, "What's in it for me?" for your followers. Advertising a service or program without promoting its benefits is counterproductive and can actually drain your library's social capital. It's very likely that your patrons are overwhelmed with input from various sources throughout their day and are suffering from information fatigue. Most have learned to be picky and are likely to tune out things they find irrelevant or equivalent to pure advertising.

Monitor and Respond to Posts

Social media serves especially well as a listening post to find out what people are saying about your library. When someone says something about your library, whether positive or negative, it's crucial to respond with *something.* Acknowledging the other person and demonstrating that your library is listening (and cares) is extremely important in building one-to-one relationships.

BOTTOM LINE ▶ Every time your library directly engages with someone online in a positive way, especially one that benefits the other person, it gains social capital. Social capital takes time to earn and trust to build.

ADVANCED SOCIAL CAPITAL STRATEGIES

Once your library has been around the social media block a few times, it may be ready to move on to some bolder methods for gaining capital and strengthening relationships. Your library may want to try some of these strategies.

Post Photos

Get an account on a Twitter-enabled service, such as Twitpic or Instagram, that allows you to post photos from anywhere and share them through your library's Twitter account. Think about putting up not only photos of events or programs but also casual or funny shots of staff going about their daily work (or perhaps celebrating a staff birthday). Photos can also add to the "humanness" of the library online and add variety to what would normally be only a stream of text posts.

Provide Good Customer Service

Social media, as a medium, is not always ideal for regular reference services. Chances are good that your library will occasionally encounter requests for help via social media, however. Some people prefer to communicate via Facebook message or Twitter tweet. Respect that these people want to communicate with the library and respond, as best as possible, using the same medium.

Promote Contests

If your library runs contests, announce the winners via social media in addition to any other avenues you might use. Try a contest done entirely via social media, such as creating online videos or captioning a photo on Flickr.

Add Social Media URLs to Business Cards and Signage

Nowadays, most libraries have their website URL included on their business cards, stationery, ads, and signs. Include your social media URLs in offline promotional materials as well. This acts as proof of social engagement, welcoming patrons to your community and building trust in your library. Integrating online and offline advertising not only is common sense but also increases your library's credibility in the social online realms.

Create a Viral Experience

One of the best examples of viral marketing is described by the Twittown blog:

> When the San Francisco area's most famous (er, only) Korean BBQ Take-Out Truck rolls into the neighborhood, lines literally stretch around the block. But given the mobile nature of the business, how do people know when and where to find it? Enter Twitter. Kogi BBQ uses Twitter to let their customers know where they are going to be each day, and if the photographs showing hundreds of people waiting in line for Korean BBQ To-Go are any indicator, it's a business strategy that has worked out incredibly well for them. The real-time nature of their business demands a real-time communications platform to underpin it, and Twitter (as well as Facebook) is the basis for that platform. Sandwich carts around the country should take note.[1]

How many libraries have bookmobiles? This is a strategy that could easily be duplicated. Using social media or texting, the library could create real-time updates and commentary along the bookmobile's route.

Social media participants have to be aware of their deposits and withdrawals of social capital. Having a healthy balance is integral to being successful in the long term. Deposits of social capital add value to the community as a whole; withdrawals only have value to the library.

> **BOTTOM LINE** Participate in conversations. Remember that the recipients of any of your library's messages have expectations of reciprocity.

Your library needs to keep a careful eye on its social capital balance to avoid becoming overdrawn.

SPENDING SOCIAL CAPITAL

Ben McConnell, a writer for the Church of the Customer blog (www.churchof customer.com) recommends a social capital deposit/withdrawal ratio of 80 to 20 percent; the vast majority of an individual's or organization's social media interactions need to be other-centered.[2]

Knowing that social capital should be spent only when necessary, you should ration it for only critical purposes. Promoting every program going on at your library will quickly run your social media account into overdraft status. Self-promotion is expensive. The Save Ohio Libraries campaign drew heavily on the social capital of a handful of individuals who were already well invested in social media communities. Advocacy is certainly one legitimate use for social capital. Some other worthwhile purposes include the following:

- Breaking news ("Sorry, the Internet is down—we're working on it!")
- Feedback ("What do you think of the new self-checkout machines?")
- Informal polls ("Which is better: storytimes on weekends or weeknights? Why?")

Yes, promote the library's programs, but advertise just those that are high-profile or that you know are a great match for your social media audience.

BOTTOM LINE ▶   Every time your library promotes something or asks for a favor, it is making a withdrawal. If your withdrawals exceed your deposits, your library effectively becomes a community leech—and in some cases, a pariah. Spend social capital wisely.

NOTES

1.   Twittown, "Five Wickedly Clever Ways to Use Twitter," October 26, 2009, http:// twittown.com/social-networks/social-networks-blog/five-wickedly-clever-ways-use -twitter.

2.   Ben McConnell, "The Last Temptation of Twitter," *Church of the Customer Blog*, December 19, 2008, www.churchofcustomer.com/2008/12/an-8020-rule-for -selfpromotion.html.

STRATEGIES FOR
SOCIAL MEDIA SUCCESS

Social media is a long sell process. You are developing
content in order to gain an order of trust with people
in your area of influence. We are now experiencing a
relationship driven economy . . . get on the train.

—KYLE LACY, AUTHOR OF *TWITTER MARKETING FOR DUMMIES*

Warren Sukernek, a social media strategist, tells the story of how he made a reservation at a hotel for a family vacation to Disneyland. He later discovered that the hotel had a Twitter account and even offered a better rate for Twitter users. Sukernek quickly changed his reservation and got the better rate. He sent a tweet to the hotel to inform them of his arrival and thank them for the great discount. To his surprise, he got no response. Once at the hotel, he received excellent service and had very nice accommodations. He even tweeted this. Still no response.

What Sukernek's story demonstrates is a common failure in social media: the misconception that it's merely a way to broadcast messages or promotions. Despite his overall favorable experience at the hotel, Sukernek no doubt felt let down that the hotel didn't want (or care) to actually converse with him via Twitter. Considering that the hotel actually had a Twitter account and Sukernek was advocating for its brand via that medium, it's surprising that the hotel did not have a follow-up plan for engaging with customers. Whether by benign neglect or deliberate omission, when communication is only one way, it demonstrates that the party initiating the message doesn't want or really care about a response. Perhaps that wasn't the intent of the hotel in Sukernek's anecdote, but the effect was the same: the hotel lost a prime opportunity to build a one-to-one relationship with one of its new customers simply by its apparent ignorance of customer expectations in social media.

There are a good number of social media best practices, some of which I discuss below. Become familiar with them and implement them at your library.

SOCIAL MEDIA PROFILES

One common element of all social media sites is the ability for participants to include some personal information about themselves. The amount and type may vary but nearly all allow for at least a name, a location, a website URL, and an avatar (image). Some have additional fields, such as a short bio, interests, and contact information. Regardless of what options are available, make sure that your library fills out all the information and in as much detail as it possibly can. Potential friends and followers will look at profiles in order to determine whether they want your library in their network.

Always remember *why* your library is in this space — to connect with others. How many people will want to connect with something that they cannot readily identify as authentic or relevant?

Your library's profile is, in many cases, the main opportunity it will have in a particular network to establish trust. The burden of credibility is on you, so being as complete as possible is key. All too often libraries fail to include simple things such as their logo. (Don't use a photo of your building; library buildings are almost never the same as a brand, and many avatars will be displayed at too small a size to show any real identifying details.)

Once you have your library's profiles set up, move on to the following "next steps."

Get a Vanity URL

On Facebook, once your library's page has twenty-five or more fans, you can convert the long, unwieldy default URL into something easy to remember, such as www.facebook.com/examplelibrary. This makes it infinitely easier for interested patrons to find your library. Add this URL to your library's print promotional materials and business cards. Also add a direct link using the Facebook logo on your library's blogs and websites.

Link Your Profiles

Some (not all) social media sites allow you to connect your accounts. For example, you can synchronize your Twitter updates to your Facebook posts (using third-party applications), so you only have to post in one place and it shows up in two. LinkedIn has various applications to import your status updates from other sites as well. This strategy not only simplifies your library's social media work, but it can also help cross-promote the library's various social media presences. Your focus should still be on customizing content for the audience, however, because using this kind of shortcut may undermine your efforts with people who choose to follow the library in more than one way online.

Install Applications

Some sites, such as Facebook and LinkedIn, allow you to customize a profile with various types of add-ons, or apps. Some are useful, and some are just for fun. You will likely find some apps that are useful for making your profile more interesting or more interactive. Apps that highlight PowerPoint applications or videos from your library can provide additional content for fans. Visual content (images and videos) also tend to have a better chance of being seen in social network feeds.

Customize Your Profile Pages

Sites such as Twitter and MySpace allow users to create custom backgrounds for their profile pages. Be sure to take full advantage of this feature by using your library's logo clearly in the background image.

BOTTOM LINE ▸   As library staff, we know that people do judge books by their covers. Your library's social media profiles are "covers" that people will use to judge the library. Put effort into making them interesting, authentic, and inviting.

LURK BEFORE YOU LEAP:
LEARNING THE COMMUNITY

When attending an event, it is the rare individual who can simply rush in and start chatting with the first person he or she encounters. Most people are likely to survey the crowd for a bit first in order to get a feel for any group dynamics that might be in play. This instinct is a particularly good one when it comes to social media. Once your library has set up its account on a given service, take some time to get the "lay of the land." Even if you have some experience with other social media networks, you may be surprised to learn that the customs of one are not necessarily the same as another. For example, what your library does on Twitter will likely be significantly different from what it does on Facebook. Twitter is excellent for sharing breaking news, while Facebook is significantly better for longer posts and for publicizing upcoming events and anecdotes that may interest others.

One way to illustrate this is to do a comparison of popular social media sites Facebook and Twitter. Many people use both, because each serves a different purpose and has different customs. Looking at table 4.1, it might be simple to guess where it would be best to promote a program that is happening in the next several weeks, as compared with announcing an Internet service outage. There is certainly overlap in users between the two services, but people will tailor their posts to the medium. A researcher at Microsoft Research New England, danah boyd (she legally changed her name to all lowercase letters), ponders the differences on her blog:

> Different social media spaces have different norms. You may not be able to describe them, but you sure can feel them. Finding the space that clicks with you is often tricky, just as finding a voice in a new setting can be. This is not to say that one space is better than the other. I don't believe that at all. But I do believe that Facebook and Twitter are actually quite culturally distinct and that trying to create features to bridge them won't actually resolve the cultural differences.[1]

As tempting as it might be to jump right in, it may be better to first observe the conversational syntaxes happening around you on these sites (see table 4.1). This may well save your library from committing an egregious faux pas.

BOTTOM LINE ▶ If your library chooses to participate in more than one social network, be sure it understands the different cultures and uses of each. Social media communities have different expectations of communication.

TABLE 4.1 **Comparison of Facebook and Twitter**

Facebook	Twitter
■ Best for connecting with people you already know	■ Best for connecting with people you don't know
■ Better for posts that are not time sensitive	■ Better for time-sensitive posts
■ Better for local news/events	■ Better for content that is not localized
■ Conversations happen less in real time	■ Conversations happen more in real time
■ Can post updates that are fairly wordy	■ Limited to 140-character updates
■ More emphasis on deep connections	■ More emphasis on follower counts
■ Complex functionality; somewhat more difficult to use	■ Simple functionality; easier to use
■ Has replaced e-mail and IM for many	■ Has replaced RSS for many

TRUST: BEING TRANSPARENT

At its core, building relationships is all about building trust. Trust can only come when both parties are open about what they are doing and what they are feeling. This means participating in social media truly necessitates being transparent. People who connect with your library often will want to know more about what's going on behind the scenes—they're looking for a more personal experience. The more you can give them that experience, the deeper the sense of connection there may be.

Continuous, open communications are an important part of developing a relationship. But how can a library do this? Here are a few suggestions.

Find Your Library's Voice

Remember that people are viewing your library as yet another node in their social network. This means it's essentially the equivalent of any other person in that network. So talk like a person! Be human. Ditch the institutional jargon. Get rid of the formal tone. Social media is much more casual than most other forms of communication. Ideally, your library will have one person doing its social media work, so that the library's voice will be consistent. However, if more than one person contributes, be sure that all of the participants understand the kind of language that will constitute online communications.

Talk About the Challenges of Your Library

It's often easier to put on a good face and only give people the upbeat or inspiring news. But we live in a world filled with difficult news as well. Show both sides of your library's "personality" by sharing issues that may be challenging. Let people know the library is worried that the upcoming levy may not pass. Tell them you're just as annoyed by the self-check machines being down as they are. Show that there are human beings behind the profile who have feelings and frustrations. Be careful, though, not to let this avenue turn into a steady stream of complaints or seem overly solicitous.

Explain Changes

Did your library have to stop buying some materials due to budget cuts? Were new self-check machines installed? Whatever the situation, use social media not only to inform but also to explain and clarify. One business owner I know will spend whatever time is needed to explain the reasoning behind even minor decisions to his employees. Over time, he has found that it helps them to empathize with the store's position if customers complain and helps them feel a part of the business. Take the time to give as much information as is reasonably possible and let your patrons feel that they are a part of the discussion.

Own Up to Your Mistakes

One of the most important parts of being transparent is being honest. If you give out incorrect information, make a public correction and apologize clearly for the error. If your library does something that garners negative feedback, don't try to hide from it. Address it directly and publicly. Organizations make mistakes, just as people do. Stand out from the crowd by coming clean about them.

Talk About Individual Staff

"Did you know that Susan, the storytime lady, is a competitive salsa dancer? We didn't know either until last week!" Or, "Thank goodness for Jim, who knows how to do a mail merge in OpenOffice." (Of course, be sure that you have permission from the staff members you want to post about.) Let people see behind the scenes and connect to individuals in your library.

BOTTOM LINE ▸ Be human and talk like a human in your social media interactions. Be authentic and honest, and connections and conversations will follow.

MAKE AN EFFORT TO UNDERSTAND YOUR ONLINE PATRONS

Just like any other form of patron interaction, understanding the audience is crucial. Regardless of what social media network your library chooses, some characteristics of its users will remain generally the same. Keeping these things in mind will help your library be more effective in the social media space.

People Are Busy—REALLY Busy

This is part of the appeal of social media: People can stay connected to those they know without having to sacrifice large blocks of time. Be sure whatever you post is worth the time of the people who will read it. This comes back to the idea of adding value when you participate in social media.

In addition, be aware that constant status updates can be interpreted as spam behavior. I have seen libraries put out a stream of five or more consecutive tweets in the morning, all promoting programs, and then nothing—no interaction and nothing later in the day. Not only was there no value to these tweets for me or even the average follower, but there also were so many so close together that I began to tune them out. With some of these libraries, I felt forced to "unfollow" them, as they simply filled up my Twitter stream with useless messages.

Time is a valuable commodity these days for everyone. Just because a library is a not-for-profit organization with loyal patrons is no excuse for overwhelming fans and followers. Show people you value their time, and they will be more likely to value your library in return.

People Want to Look Good

When people can share something unique and interesting with their network of friends, it helps them to accumulate social capital. Every time that your library's posts can help someone look like they are smart, have special status, or are "in the know," it's a win-win situation. That person looks good to friends, and your library gets social capital as the result of having done a favor. In addition, the library has helped start a conversation.

If the library reposts something someone else on the network has said (e.g., retweeting), that makes people look good, too. It is a direct affirmation of the worth of the content's originator.

BOTTOM LINE No matter what social network your library chooses to participate in, always remember that people appreciate the value of content. Don't waste people's time with posts or status updates that are just worthless fillers.

RESPONSE TIME MATTERS
MORE THAN YOU MAY THINK

In April 2009, Amazon.com apologized to Twitter users after the sales rankings and some search results for gay and lesbian literature quietly disappeared from the merchant's site. The apology came after a tremendous online uproar with much negative criticism of Amazon and unfriendly commentary about Amazon's new label of "adult" for the genre. The social media backlash was obviously unexpected by the online retailer. What was more surprising, however, was the further and extensive criticism leveled at Amazon for its slow response time to the concerns of its customers. When Amazon failed to respond to commentary within a day, the social media world emphatically labeled the company as uncommunicative.

Companies and organizations are learning, much to their chagrin, that communication is now 24/7. It used to be, with traditional offline media, that if a crisis happened on a Friday, you likely had the weekend to think about a response and then could implement that response the following Monday. In the social media world, twenty-four hours is a *very* long time. Amazon.com could have avoided at least some of the backlash simply by communicating more quickly; it failed to consider that the accelerated time frame within which social media operates can turn a relatively routine incident into a marketing crisis.

Social media happens in real or almost-real time. Participating in conversations as they happen is an absolute must for the successful organization today. Preventing a marketing crisis is not the only reason to monitor social media constantly, however. For a library, timeliness is more likely to come into play when responding to simple questions or comments. Don't let even positive posts wait! Just as your fans and followers want your content, they also want your

Response time is absolutely critical in social media, especially when dealing with something negative.

attention. When they don't get it in what they perceive to be a timely manner, chances are good they'll feel rejected and may even cease connecting at all (e.g., unfriending or unfollowing).

BOTTOM LINE ▸ Social media, in many cases, is happening in close to real time. Failure to respond promptly to a conversation, either positive or negative, can result in a great deal of harm to your library's reputation.

FORMING A LIBRARY "FRIENDING" POLICY

In earlier days of social media, it was not uncommon to see libraries with social media accounts where the library had only allowed other libraries, librarians, or perhaps authors to be "friends" of the account. Often, this was a misguided attempt to somehow gain control in a medium that is inherently very open. Sometimes, it was a lack of understanding on the part of a library's board or administrators about what social media really is.

Unfortunately, misperceptions still persist. Once, I was contacted by a frustrated librarian whose library had a MySpace account. The librarian friended anyone who wanted to be MySpace friends, believing that the library should be accessible to all. It later turned out that some of the friends had questionable content on their profiles. The administration reacted by severely criticizing the librarian and shutting down the entire account.

This particular reaction raises several important issues:

- Part of the administration's overreaction was likely due to a misconception about how to approach social media. Traditional marketing and reputation management resolutions are not applicable. Libraries need to understand that successful social media has a human tone. Being human means having human friends, not necessarily paragons of what we may expect our patrons to be.
- Another likely reason for this response may have resulted from a misunderstanding of what the term *friend* means in social media. The word does not have the same connotations as it does offline, and rarely does it refer to an actual close, personal bond.
- Whatever is on a person's profile reflects on that person and not necessarily on the connecting friends. Unless the profile is somehow directly harming the library's reputation, there is no reason to believe the library is somehow responsible for this content. After all, we are not personally responsible for every silly picture or off-the-wall comment that our friends post online.
- A library is a public space and thus open to everyone. Why would the library screen patrons at its virtual door who would be free to enter its physical one? Why would the library's presence online only be open to some people and not to all?

Stories like this one serve to emphasize there is a great deal of confusion in libraries about how to handle actual connections (friends, followers, fans, etc.)

in social media. Who *should* a library connect to? Who should it avoid? Should it be a completely open online forum? There are no truly hard-and-fast rules to follow in this regard. Table 4.2 shows some important criteria libraries can use to guide them in forming their own friending policies.

TABLE 4.2 **Friending guidelines**

Keep	Ignore/Block
■ Business or organization in your library's service area	■ Business or organization that is not in your library's service area or has nothing to do with libraries
■ People, even if they are not in your service area	■ People, regardless of location, who use highly sexualized avatars (these are almost always spambots, not real people)
■ People who mention the library online	■ People or organizations that are overly self-promotional or constantly trying to sell something

What about the idea of only connecting to other libraries or librarians? As mentioned previously, this is an outdated approach. There are three main problems with this: (1) it discriminates against anyone who's not in a "library" category; (2) it will be immediately apparent when potential friends/followers look at your library's profile that it is a closed forum; and (3) perhaps most significant, it totally ignores the whole precept of social media—to connect to a community at large.

Another common problem I've encountered (especially on Twitter) is the library that follows *no one* back. These are likely libraries that believe social media is just another way to broadcast their message, and it indicates a tremendous failure to understand the potential of the medium. Not making any connections also shows the library has no interest in listening to its patrons—not a message any institution would want to send, even inadvertently. Make sure your follower ratio is somewhat even, that your library follows back roughly the same number of people following it.

BOTTOM LINE ▸ Connect to people who want to connect to you, unless you have a very good reason not to. Your library cannot be judged by the actions of an individual who is not an actual employee of the library.

DON'T ABANDON YOUR FANS

Social media takes time, work, and a sense of commitment. It's something that must be tended to daily, and with care. Once your library starts acquiring friends and followers, there is an unspoken obligation to communicate regularly with them. People friend/follow with the assumption that your library will be imparting content of some interest to them.

Eventually, some of these followers will fall off to pursue other interests. However, if your library fails to post regularly, it will lose followers much more quickly, in much the same way that an apparently abandoned blog will lose readership. Use both status updates and varied conversations with followers to maintain a constant stream of communication.

BOTTOM LINE▸   Failing to use existing social media accounts is a direct failure of communication with your library's friends and followers.

EMPOWERING LIBRARY STAFF

This is something that can be especially difficult for library administrators to grasp. They are not alone; many for-profit workplaces restrict access to social media by employees, mistakenly believing this will somehow allow the company to control what employees do and say during work hours. Inevitably, these employees find ways around such restrictions and may end up saying more negative things about their place of employment than they might have otherwise.

Smart organizations have come to realize empowered employees make for powerful and effective social media channels. Zappos.com is often cited as a company that gets social media right; it not only uses Twitter effectively to build its customer base but also actively encourages its employees to tweet. Tony Hsieh, the CEO of Zappos.com, says this of his company's Twitter policy: "I think it's important for employees to be able to express their individuality. We want our customers to feel like they are interacting with real people, not a faceless corporation."[2] Undoubtedly, this will make some people leery. Won't staff waste inordinate amounts of time on social media? Kyle Lacy, the author of *Twitter Marketing for Dummies*, says:

It is time to stop being afraid of the massive force of online communication. It is time to stop putting firewalls up because you're afraid your employees are not being productive. They are not being productive for a reason . . . and it's not Facebook. If they love what they do . . . maybe it is time to allow them to communicate that fact . . . and if they don't . . . you probably have more problems than communication.[3]

If your library would like to follow in the footsteps of Tony Hsieh, you can encourage staff to share specific types of content. Some of these might include:

- *Events.* Suggest that staff help promote major (not minor) events. Employees should also indicate if they are attending.
- *Awards.* If your library receives a community award or is ranked highly by such surveys as Hennepin or *Library Journal*'s 5-Star Libraries, ask employees to help spread the word. They can help make your local community proud of its library.
- *Extraordinary promotions.* If your library does something like "Food for Fines," staff could help get the news out. Think of this kind of post as something done maybe three or four times a year, or the novelty will wear off quickly.
- *New blog post.* This isn't to suggest that you ask your staff to promote every new post on the library blog. Rather, ask them to point to blog posts that might be very unusual (e.g., penned by the director) or to those written by third-party individuals that might mention some aspect of the library.
- *New services.* If your library starts doing something both new and on a large scale (e.g., switching to self-check machines), this is a prime opportunity for staff to talk about it and reassure their followers about any concerns.
- *Videos.* Videos can have very powerful click-through rates (especially if they're funny). If your library makes videos for either instruction or entertainment, staff could assist in getting them seen.

BOTTOM LINE   Your library's employees can be a powerful set of connections. Use them to make your library more human, but use them sparingly.

DECIDING WHO'S IN CHARGE

There is much debate about exactly who should control an organization's social media presence. Even in the corporate world, there is not a clearly defined answer. In many cases, companies have decided that their public relations staff should manage social media: not only does their title include the word *public,* but they likely possess expertise in speaking to the public without jargon and in clear, concise language. However, this argument doesn't necessarily work for libraries, where the majority of the staff probably works with the public on a daily basis. In fact, one of the most common complaints I hear from librarians is that their library's social media is controlled by the PR department—and the kinds of communication that appear in the library's social media are self-serving, stiff, or even arrogant.

Who's right? And what about the teen librarian? How about the IT department? Some even consider their human resources staff for the job. Obviously, there is not a cut-and-dried answer to this question.

Mary Deming Barber, communications consultant at the Barber Group, says: "Social media is about engagement and conversation, neither of which are strengths of IT or HR. Beyond that, the decision to place 'control' in PR, marketing, communications or other seems to be based on an individual company and its structure."[4]

Barber nails the main issue: social media is about engagement and conversation. The person responsible for the library's social media needs to excel at this. This will not automatically mean the PR person, teen librarian, or any particular position in the library. It's not about title or position. Your library may have a reference librarian handling social media for several months, only to have that person leave. Rather than automatically giving it to the reference librarian's replacement, the successful library will evaluate the staff as a whole to see who is best suited for the job. Does this mean that the maintenance guy could be doing the tweeting? Possibly! The answer to the question of who's in charge of a library's social media is truly situational.

BOTTOM LINE ▶ Don't assign social media work to someone based on title or how some other library has delegated the job. Make sure the person you choose is the right fit for the job.

IS A SOCIAL MEDIA "EXPERT" THE ANSWER?

Recently, there have been some comparisons between the appearance of self-proclaimed social media experts, or "gurus," and the advent of the dot-boom era. During the early part of the first decade of the twenty-first-century, many companies believed that a fancy website or putting ".com" after their name was an automatic ticket to success. Many such organizations learned, too late, that neither strategy was a surefire way to gain customer business or loyalty. A good number of such businesses failed. In more recent times, we are seeing organizations latch onto so-called social media professionals, rather than using web designers. Instead of banking on fancy websites, this time organizations are relying on people who claim expertise in a field that has only existed in its current form for less than a decade.

Peter Shankman, social media entrepreneur and CEO of The Geek Factory, Inc., a boutique social media, marketing, and PR strategy firm located in New York City, describes this phenomenon:

> We got thirsty again, and are drinking the same damn ten-year-old Kool-Aid without so much as asking for ice. Rather than embracing this new technology and merging it with what we've learned already, we're throwing off our clothes and running naked in the rain, waving our hands in the air, sure that this time it'll be different, because this time it's better!![5]

Shankman is known for his unique and frank posts on social media as an industry. In his blog post "I Will Never Hire a 'Social Media Expert,' and Neither Should You," he points out the fallacy of this kind of thinking. Social media's bottom line is about generating revenue and providing excellent customer service: that's what any interaction, online or off, has been about since the beginning of time. If the person your library hires or appoints to do its social media work cannot accomplish these kinds of goals, it's not going to matter how cute or funny his or her posts are. In the end, social media is about meeting goals using a certain type of tool. It's not about how cool your library thinks social media is.

Ideally, your library is likely going to want to have someone on staff handling its social media efforts. An outside professional can still be of use to your library, if you're looking for further guidance on setting goals, figuring ROI, or strategies for specific campaigns. The most recent trend is for organizations to use someone inside the organization to do most or all of the social media work. Internal employees often know the library best, and may know how best to handle certain inquiries and individuals, or how to avoid particular political minefields in their community. This kind of knowledge is invaluable, and usually cannot be replicated by an outside consultant.

BOTTOM LINE ▸ Outside social media consultants may be useful to gain direction, but are usually not a good fit as replacements for a library staff member who has internal knowledge of the library and its relationships with its community.

WHAT QUALITIES SHOULD A SOCIAL MEDIA COORDINATOR HAVE?

Remember, the qualities a social media coordinator needs may or may not be found in a particular job position. Keep an open mind and consider the following as desired characteristics:

- *Passion.* Enthusiasm is a must, since real social media work can quickly become tedious. Whoever does this work for your library should *want* to do it.
- *Organizational knowledge.* The selected person should be someone who has been at the library for a significant amount of time. He or she should have a strong sensitivity to the library's politics and a strong sense of its history. This will prove invaluable when dealing with customer service issues and for knowing what is and is not appropriate to post.
- *A grounded personality.* While enthusiasm is crucial, it won't compensate for a lack of understanding concerning the realities of the work. The library staff member who evangelizes about social media is not necessarily going to prioritize ROI over "cool." In the end, it will be results that matter. This person may not possess a true understanding of how time-consuming the work is, or how important it is for the library's social media presence to be consistent.
- *Brevity.* Social media is probably not the best job for the staff member who writes novels in his or her spare time. As a means of communication, social media requires that as few words as possible are used to create messages, not only because of site-imposed limits (e.g., Twitter's 140-character limit) but also because of the

incredibly limited amount of attention any one posted item is likely to receive.

- *Good writing skills.* It's not just about keeping posts short; they also have to be clear and free of spelling and grammatical errors. Yes, social media is more casual, but do you *really* want your library represented by someone who doesn't know the difference between *lose* and *loose*?
- *Familiarity with the library's patrons—or willingness to get to know them.* Knowing the kinds of people who frequent or contact the library can help immensely. Even if the person doesn't know patrons well, he or she needs to be willing to learn. Shankman says:

> Do you know your audience? Have you reached out to them? I'm not talking about "tweeting at them," I'm talking about actually reaching out. Asking them what you can do better? Asking those who haven't been around in a while what you can do to get them back? It's not about 10% off coupons or "contests for the next follower." For God's sake, be smarter than that.[6]

True social media work is about forging relationships with your library's patrons. This person has to be willing to do what's needed to get to that goal, even if it's uncomfortable.

- *Customer advocacy.* The person the library chooses to represent it online should clearly show an understanding that one of their main responsibilities is to *help* patrons. In this sense, the work is not much different from assisting patrons in the physical library. Superior service is one of the ways that libraries can use social media to their advantage. It's important that social media coordinators take this to heart and prioritize the needs of patrons over their own sensitivities.

BOTTOM LINE ▸ The person your library selects to be its online voice needs not only enthusiasm but also an informed perspective about what the work actually entails.

STATUS UPDATE MAKEOVERS

Up until now, we've discussed many ways that libraries can make their use of social media more effective. However, we haven't really looked at concrete examples of both good and bad uses of social media. In this section, we'll look at some examples of social status updates and why they are problematic. I'll also show some ways that these same updates can be remade to be more appealing and more effective.

The Internet computers are not
available due to maintenance.

Why Is This Ineffective?

This update sounds like it came from a robot. It's highly impersonal and is likely to be ignored, turn people off, or both. "Maintenance" is not descriptive and doesn't really say what's going on. In this example, it constitutes generic language.

How Could It Be Better?

People want to know there is a human being behind the account. The only way to do that is to use language that demonstrates a real person is making the post. Remember, part of the reason people will connect to your library is to get more behind-the-scenes information. Give some detail. Transparency is important.

REMADE EXAMPLE ONE

Argh! Power surge took down a server—
no Internet here this morning, sorry!

Why Is This Better?

It's easy to tell with the addition of expressive language (i.e., "Argh!") that a real person, with real emotions, is making the post. Additional information is provided that really explains why there is no Internet access at the library today. The simple addition of the word sorry at the end of the post shows that the library is sympathetic to those who may have wanted to come in to use the Internet.

Helped a patron find a turnip cookbook today.

Why Is This Ineffective?

Whenever the library makes a status update, it has to consider how it will be received. One question to continually ask is, What's in this post for someone else? Another question to ask would be, Why should someone else care? The cookbook in question may have been unique or fascinating, but there's no sense of that in the post. For all the end user knows, requests for turnip cookbooks could be routine in a library. There's nothing to indicate this is an unusual request.

How Could It Be Better?

More detail is required to really make this post stand out and possibly spark a conversation. Including a few extra words to help put the comment into context will help.

REMADE EXAMPLE TWO

Helped patron find turnip cookbook.
Didn't know there was such a thing!

Why Is This Better?

The main thing that makes this different from the original is the addition of the second sentence. It lets the reader know the cookbook was unique enough to pique the interest of the librarian. It also shows a sense of transparency and openness; the librarian is showing he or she doesn't know everything. Lastly, it adds a very human touch to an otherwise unremarkable post.

Cool sailboat craft program at 10 am today!

Why Is This Ineffective?

This status update is fairly typical of most libraries currently using Twitter purely as a broadcast mechanism. The update does nothing beyond promote a program. It gives no reason why anyone would want to attend other than because the library has declared it to be "cool." There is no clue as to the payoff for the reader.

How Could It Be Better?

The subject matter of the craft session (i.e., sailboats) isn't really what the reader will get out of the program. In fact, the reader in this case is not the potential participant but rather the parent. Gear the message accordingly. What will parents get out of it? Why should they bring their kids?

REMADE EXAMPLE THREE

It's noisy, messy, and chaotic, & your kids will love it! Crafts @ 10 am today.

Why Is This Better?

The payoff is much more readily apparent; it's a program with qualities that will be fun for kids, and if parents bring their children, the kids will love the program. Note that the subject of the crafts needn't even be included in such a brief announcement; people will be primarily interested in what they will get out of it. There's also a possibility the lack of craft subject may inspire fans or followers to respond with additional questions, initiating further conversation around the topic and potentially garnering interest from others.

New science fiction and fantasy
books at your library [LINK].

Why Is This Ineffective?

Much like the previous example, this status update is primarily self-promotional. Aside from that, it's pretty blasé as a status update. It lacks any interesting framework to catch the attention of busy followers. Even a hard-core genre fan may overlook this particular announcement.

How Could It Be Better?

Always remember that your library's fans may be extremely busy, so compose status updates to make it worth their while to read them. Connect the announcement in some way to something that gives it more context.

REMADE EXAMPLE FOUR

New Nebula Award winners just announced!
Request copies at [LINK].

Why Is This Better?

This status update serves two functions: it gives breaking news ("Nebula Award winners just announced!"), and it informs interested followers that items in a particular genre are available. It provides additional context for the post that is more likely to gain attention. This strategy has been extended by explaining to readers that the link in the posting will take them directly to the new science fiction and fantasy selections where they can browse and request these titles.

*Next week at the library: HOMEWORK
HELP CENTER [LINK].*

Why Is This Ineffective?

This particular status post is, overall, very uninformative. It makes an assumption that the reader will bother to click through the link in order to get any real information about the program. Keep in mind readers will only click a link if you have caught their interest first. Just because a post is from their local library isn't reason enough to assume fans are tempted by anything it has to say. All-caps usage is also troubling. It is a well-known convention on the Web that all-caps indicate shouting; no fan wants to be yelled at.

How Could It Be Better?

Once again, it's important to give the readers something they want. Readers might want a homework help center, but it would be difficult to know for sure without specifics. Also, because the post originates with a library's social media account, there's not likely to be a need to announce the location of the help center.

REMADE EXAMPLE FIVE

*Kids getting worried about report
cards? Homework Help Center begins
on Monday @ 4:00 pm [LINK].*

Why Is This Better?

The remade version provides additional context that will help a potential reader decide if he or she is interested in the update. The hook is clear (kids + report cards = worry) and implies the nature of the payoff: kids will get help that may result in better grades. Including a specific date and time is also beneficial, as it gives more information up front without making the reader do more work to get it.

MAGAZINES AS ROLE MODELS

One of the best examples for how to do status updates well may come from near the checkout at your local grocery store. The next time you visit, take a careful look at some of the headlines that beckon from the covers of many of the magazines displayed in the racks:

- "Walk Off 10 Pounds in 10 Days"
- "What to Wear Now"
- "Get Back Your Shape"
- "15 Tips for a Bigger Tax Refund"
- "Smart Clothes for Tough Times"
- "How to Look 10 Years Younger"
- "Simple Ways to Declutter Every Room"

Why do magazines use these kinds of headlines? In a word: economy. Not only do they have a limited amount of space on the cover, they also know they have a very brief time in which to capture a potential buyer's attention. In order to tempt someone to buy their publication, magazine editors know that headlines need to be short and sweet and the payoff very clear.

Libraries are actually dealing with a very similar situation, where limited amount of space is available for most status updates and the attention span of potential readers is often very short by necessity. Yet most libraries fail to capture the attention of their audience because they tend to mistake a status update with a call for action. It's vital for successful long-term use of social media to remember that a call to action draws on social capital. Therefore, nearly every time your library specifically asks followers to exert an effort, especially toward a particular goal of the library (by doing, being, having, checking, joining, seeing, hearing, or coming), that is a withdrawal, not a deposit. Most calls to action don't have anything of inherent value to followers. Remember: calls to action represent the need to ask a favor. Your followers primarily want to know what the library can do for them, not the reverse.

BOTTOM LINE Make status updates human. Always remember what will be first and foremost in the readers' minds: the payoff. What will they get from your post? If you can't easily answer that question, rewrite the update.

THINKING ABOUT YOUTUBE?

YouTube, the world's most popular video-sharing social network, can be a difficult arena for libraries. Few libraries have the resources to create professional-looking productions, and fewer still can achieve the viral success sought after by so many. The Harold B. Lee Library, the main library at Brigham Young University, has surely been the envy of many libraries after its successful and viral video, *Study Like a Scholar, Scholar,* which was a parody of a popular video campaign by Old Spice. It has been viewed nearly three million times. The Lee Library is fortunate in having in-house expertise that allows it to create polished products. This may not be the case with the majority of other libraries, who may not have internal or skilled specialists.

The Worthington Libraries in Ohio provide an example that may help other libraries consider how best to approach using YouTube. This public library system has had mixed results with their YouTube content, with the number of views ranging from 200 to over 300,000. Kara Reuter, the library's digital library manager, learned lot of what she needed to know on the job and has some useful information from her experiences to share.

- *Guessing what's going to be popular can be difficult.* Reuter notes that they have not found an audience for many of their videos. In one instance, the library produced a three-part video about *Star Wars* collectibles, believing that it would have no trouble getting viewers. The series received less than 1,000 total views, while, surprisingly, their flannel board storytime series has averaged close to 40,000 views apiece, with one featuring Old MacDonald getting more than 335,000 views. One lesson Reuter learned from this experience is to question whether or not a video idea will have wide appeal. Reuter herself has watched the flannel board storytimes on her phone with her own baby and suspects that many parents may do the same. The storytimes are great entertainment for very young children and can be watched on mobile devices, which likely contributed to their popularity. Be sure to ask, "Who is this video serving?"
- *Some programs are better for videos than others.* Worthington Libraries found that not only storytimes but also author visits provide better material and venues for video production. Reuter's advice for library videos is, "If you can't do it on a tripod, don't do it!" If a program requires camera movement, it will usually be beyond the skills of the

amateur. Programs where someone is talking at the front of a room are ideal, as the camera can be set in one location and not moved. Candid footage, where one attempts to film people in motion or to scan the audience for reactions, is very difficult and can more likely result in poor-quality video. "It's much easier to make a bad video than a good one," says Reuter.

- *Don't underestimate the problem of people not wanting to be filmed.* Some people, both staff and the public, really don't want to appear on camera. Some speakers from outside of the library may also have reservations. Be sure to get approval (in writing if required) from anyone who could end up in your final video.

- *Be aware of some of the "gotchas" on YouTube.* Reuter describes the comments that can be made on YouTube videos as the "Wild West of the Internet." Some comments Worthington Libraries has received have been obscene or wildly inappropriate. The library does allow for comments, but approves them before allowing them to appear. Reuter points out that her library does allow negative comments, so long as they are centered on, say, the performance rather than on the performer personally. Another issue her library became aware of was that of related videos. YouTube automatically shows links to videos it thinks may be related to the one you have posted. In one case, a storytime that the library had tagged with the word *diapers* caused YouTube to recommend some diaper-fetish videos that the library didn't want to be associated with. Worthington Libraries is now careful about what words they use to tag their videos.

- *There is often a very large skill, time, and money investment involved.* To edit the videos the library produced, it purchased Adobe Premiere—a professional-level video editing software package that was fairly expensive. For Reuter, the learning curve for the software was very steep and required a great deal of time. Even once comfortable with using the software, it takes a great deal of time to actually edit a video. Allow for this when estimating production timelines and budgets.

BOTTOM LINE ▶ YouTube can be a much more challenging social media arena than many others. Be sure that your library can make all of the needed commitments before deciding whether YouTube is the right choice.

WHAT ABOUT LINKEDIN?

LinkedIn is perhaps much more specialized than any of the previously mentioned social networks, and is definitely more "professional" in nature. Not only are real names required, but also the goal is to connect to others in the real-world work environment. LinkedIn is primarily about building employment-related connections; as a result, the types of networking from socializing on LinkedIn are much less casual than most other social media sites. LinkedIn's stated goal is clear, "Get the most from your professional network." Considering the nature of LinkedIn, is there a place in libraries for its use?

Cuyahoga County Public Library (CCPL) in Ohio has found a unique niche for LinkedIn. The library maintains a career counseling center and several job clubs at various branches. In 2008, a patron member of one of the job clubs suggested using LinkedIn to help connect all of the club members to keep them abreast of other information related to job hunting. Four years later, the job club members-only group has more than 300 members, and the LinkedIn group is one of the first steps promoted to new clients of the career counseling center and job club members.

Jim Hansen, MS, PCC-S, is a career counselor for CCPL. Hansen points out that more and more employers are turning first to LinkedIn for potential employees, making it important for his job-seeking clients to have a presence there. He says that at least two members of the job club have been hired via LinkedIn alone (and were approached first by companies, not the other way around). Both Hansen and CCPL have found it to be a very effective tool for communicating relevant information to job club members; shared items include current job openings, job and career fair listings, and articles related to job hunting. Members also use the group to communicate similar information with each other. Even job club alumni who are now employed continue to share job openings with current members. LinkedIn is also a great way to do research on potential employers, says Hansen, and he encourages group members to use it for that purpose. It can also be a good tool for finding someone local who works for a particular company.

The career counselors, including Hansen, consistently monitor the group's postings for inappropriate items, such as ads from people attempting to sell things to the group's members. The group is also invite-only, making it more difficult for inappropriate items to be posted.

BOTTOM LINE ▶   LinkedIn is a much more specialized network than many others. Be sure your library has a real use for it before it jumps on board.

CASE STUDY: DOING SOCIAL MEDIA RIGHT

Columbus Metropolitan Library (CML) in Columbus, Ohio, was named *Library Journal*'s Library of the Year for 2010. While the reasons for this award were many, surely one factor had to be the savvy use of social media. With knowledgeable planning and execution, CML was able to increase the number of people who "like" the library on Facebook from 3,000 to more than 15,000 in less than six months,[7] and as of this writing now has more than 18,000. Its Twitter account boasts a healthy following of over 5,000 followers and is listed more than 450 times. While the number of friends or followers does not necessarily indicate success, in CML's case it certainly demonstrates that it is doing something right. What is it that CML is doing well?

- *It rarely blows its own horn.* This library recognizes that simply promoting itself is a poor use of social media. CML uses a ratio of 70/20/10: 70 percent of its online interaction is original content of value; 20 percent involves interactions with individuals; and 10 percent is pure self-promotion.
- *It is always looking for ways to interact and collaborate.* When the Columbus Zoo had a new polar bear exhibit, the library promoted the zoo's exhibit and included a link to polar bear–related items in its online catalog.
- *It's choosy about which events get a shout-out.* When its posts *are* self-promotional, the library is very selective about which events it promotes. It rarely posts storytimes: instead, the events are ones of much more general interest or larger in scale.
- *Posts are consistent.* CML tweets regularly, approximately one to five times per day. Its followers are assured of regular contact and content.
- *It has a consistent voice.* Regardless of where the library is posting or responding in social media, whatever it says has a consistent tone (and this is part of their social media policy!). They've taken this one step further: they do not have separate pages for their many branches. They present a unified front to the world with a single voice. This is far more effective than allowing each branch to maintain a presence, which almost always results in an inconsistent "feel" across a library system's pages. Having one "home" also gives people an easier way to connect, as they do not have to associate themselves with just one branch.

- *It follows back.* A common error many libraries make in Twitter is not following back where appropriate. For a public library, that means following almost everyone. Columbus Metro has also shown some marketing savvy here, which has resulted in good publicity. The library makes sure it follows the accounts of local media (radio, TV, etc.), which usually means those accounts will follow back. In one instance, CML tweeted about the large increase of people using its Homework Help centers, and a local television station contacted the library to do a news story about it.

- *It recognizes that social media monitoring is critical.* In one instance, CML was able to respond directly to an upset blogger, telling her what the library was doing to improve the situation she was angrily blogging about. If CML hadn't been listening appropriately in the social media sphere, it is unlikely that it would have ever known this person was upset with the library. Because of the monitoring, the library was able to avert a potentially bigger issue. That blogger was not only appeased, she's also now an active volunteer for the library's levy campaign.

The Columbus Metropolitan Library has also spent a significant amount of time creating and implementing a comprehensive social media strategy (see figure 4.1). This includes not only an overall planning document but also schedules of what and when they will be posting via their social media channels (see figures 4.2 and 4.3). The library's goals are clearly defined, and the staff is never stuck wondering what content they'll promote on a particular day.

NOTES

1. danah boyd, "Some Thoughts on Twitter vs. Facebook Status Updates," October 25, 2009, www.zephoria.org/thoughts/archives/2009/10/25/some_thoughts_o-3.html.

2. Shannon Nelson, "Improving Brand Value through Social Media: Zappos Gets It Right," May 15, 2008, www.piercemattiepublicrelations.com/social_networks.

3. Kyle Lacy, "Empower Your Employees to Win with Social Media," January 20, 2010, http://kylelacy.com/empower-your-employees-to-win-with-social-media.

4. Rick Alcantara, "Who Should 'Control' Social Media within a Company?" *Social Media Today*, March 22, 2010, www.socialmediatoday.com/SMC/183509.

5. Peter Shankman, "I Will Never Hire a 'Social Media Expert,' and Neither Should You." May 20, 2011. http://shankman.com/i-will-never-hire-a-social-media-expert -and-neither-should-you/.

6. Ibid.

7. Julie Theado, phone interview, August 31, 2010.

2011 SOCIAL MEDIA PLAN

SITUATION ANALYSIS:

Columbus Metropolitan Library's social media plan last year was a tremendous success. We learned a lot and exceeded expectations. For example, a year ago CML had approximately 3,500 Facebook "likes" and now we have 18,500.

We implemented some items that worked and others that didn't. For example, LinkedIn was an initiative we outlined last year, but after examining it more closely we determined not to spend much effort towards LinkedIn at the time. We felt we needed to do a few things really well and then expand in 2011.

The bar has been set high for CML's social media initiatives and the 2011 plan takes additional risks, but stays within the overall strategy of the organization. Social media can't do it alone; it must work with the organization's existing and future strategies in order to have the most impact.

This year's plan highlights some unique programs that build on our existing success and creates more opportunities for our customers.

GOALS:

- Maintain CML's presence in social media while creating unique customer experiences.
- Customize features for identified customer audiences (i.e., genealogy, small business, teens, etc.).
- Utilize social media in the rollout and launch of columbuslibrary.org.
- Continue to build relationships with local bloggers.
- Integrate Friends, Foundation and Volunteers into our communication efforts as it relates to social media.
- Locally and nationally, continue to position CML as an industry leader in social media.

TACTICS:

CML Blogs:

- We have developed strong relationships with several local bloggers and it might be interesting to allow a few guest blog posts throughout the year. For example, the book that changed Nate Rigg's life, the best cookbook from Hounds in the Kitchen, favorite children's book from CBus Mom.
- Each CML blog should have an RSS feed option so people can receive the latest blog posts in their email.
- There are several blogs that review books or discuss genealogy and we need to find a better way to develop relationships with these individuals. CML bloggers could reference one of their recent posts or profile some of their favorite blogs to read.

FIGURE 4.1 **Social media plan for Columbus Metropolitan Library. Courtesy of the Columbus Metropolitan Library, Columbus, Ohio.**

Blogger Relations:

- Research our existing blog relationships and find topics that might benefit their blogs. This would be a specific "pitch" schedule that would address their interest. For example, Andrea with Off Her Cork is going through classes to be a nutrition/life coach, are there books we can suggest? Nate Riggs focuses on the Gen Yers and building his business, is there something in SBN that might be of interest to him?
- We also think a few of the local bloggers would enjoy participating in a Ready to Read Corps Ride-a-long. Maybe we offer three ride-a-longs in one day and each blogger is paired with a Corps team.

Facebook:

- Our Facebook page has 18,500 people who have "liked" us which is a tremendous number. Our age ranges are from 13 (or younger) to 55-plus and we are currently communicating the same way to everyone. We need to find ways to customize specific information by creating custom tabs for teens, locations, kids, eReaders and volunteers.
- It is also time to survey/poll our Facebook "likes" to ensure we're providing the type of content they need/want from CML.
- Last year we ran a Facebook ad that created thousands of additional "likes" and we plan to continue to utilize Facebook ads for certain programs or areas of focus. It would be appropriate to develop a Facebook ad for Summer Reading Club or other programs. This would be customized and more specific to the demographics we're trying to reach.
- Work with Gale to add unique Facebook applications to the page in order to continue to engage customers.

Twitter:

- Develop two Tweet Chats that can engage specific customers and utilize staff expertise.
- @LibraryJennifer could host a monthly CML book club Tweet Chat where she'll be able to use her expertise on behalf of the library.
- Robin Nesbitt will host a Tweet Chat from @ColumbusLibrary account where she'll address questions involving eReaders, what's next, new books published, etc. These chats could be weekly or monthly.
- Develop specific Twitter lists that could include teen authors, book clubs, etc.
- Assist Patrick Losinski in maintaining and adding content to his Twitter account. Develop a content calendar if deemed necessary.
- Include Tweets that discuss Friends of the Library, Foundation and volunteers.

cont.

Columbuslibrary.org:
- Redesigning the website is a large initiative for CML and our social media tools can be developed so we're offering customers a unique experience.
- Develop a Facebook survey/poll to ask people who have liked us what is most important to them on our site, what would they like added or deleted, etc.
- Allow individuals on Facebook to comment and offer suggestions on a beta site.
- Solicit local bloggers such as Walker Evans and Nate Riggs to review the beta site and provide feedback.
- By leaking the site in advance, we create interest and additional attention (in the social media space) once the website officially launches.

Speaking Engagements/National Articles:
- Our social media initiatives are gaining interests locally and nationally and we need to continue to pursue ways to increase the attention and position CML as a social media leader.
- This year, we should build on this experience and find ways to present to additional industry conferences as well as those related to marketing, public relations and social media.
- We have submitted a proposal to PLA 2012 to discuss social media and will know if we've been selected in March.
- Last year, we were interviewed for books on libraries using social media and wrote a few articles regarding the topic.
- Consider submitting award entries for Public Relations Society of America (PRSA) Prism Awards or AMA's awards.
- Submitted proposal to speak at OLC's October conference regarding ways to use social media in a levy campaign.

YouTube:
- Our YouTube channel has 69 subscribers and our videos have received more than 53,000 views.
- We need to continue to provide content on YouTube because it helps share our story.
- When the redeveloped website is live, it will be important to have video uploaded there as well.

MEASUREMENT:
- This often depends on the social media tool we're using. For Twitter we can tell which tweets received the most attention and how many people clicked on one of our links.

FIGURE 4.1 **(cont.)**

- Google Analytics continues to be the tool that is preferred in order to determine traffic to our site or Facebook page. The marketing department needs access to and additional training in Google Analytics.
- In regards to the blogs, it's important that each blogger has an RSS feed so people can subscribe to receive their posts directly in their email.

ADDITIONAL APPLICATIONS:
- QR codes – CML could develop QR codes throughout certain areas of Main Library where individuals can snap a picture of the QR code in order to receive a message. This could be used with information about historic facts, library messages, promoting Summer Reading Club, etc.
- FourSquare and Facebook Places – At the very least, CML needs to claim its organization on these websites in order to maintain consistency. It is possible to add Facebook Places to our Facebook page, but by doing so we'll lose some customizable features such as a welcome page. We should continue to monitor this activity, but not invest too many resources in developing a program specific to these tools. If the right opportunity comes along, then we should find as many ways as possible to use the program.
- Groupon – Offering deals to the masses is a huge trend at the moment and while we don't often have things to sell, we could consider offering discounted Friends of the Library membership. It is typically 50% off and might create additional exposure for the Friends as well as new members. If this is something we should consider, the proposed next step would be to talk in detail to Groupon.
- Mobile apps/website – While columbuslibrary.org is being redeveloped, we should not lose track of our next steps. We should seriously consider developing a mobile app or at the very least an intuitive mobile website. While this might rest in DS/IT, marketing will play a major role in this initiative.

FUTURE MARKETING STRATEGIES:
- As we move forward on new initiatives such as health literacy, we'll need to determine how social media fits within the overall marketing strategy. Some initial thoughts would be to involve local bloggers who focus on organic cooking (Hounds in the Kitchen) or running (Off Her Cork).

twitter

TWITTER CONTENT CALENDAR

The following items are suggestions for content development for each week. This is a flexible document so if something needs to be changed or moved to a different date that is not a problem. This provides us with a starting point in order to develop and create some possible topics for discussion. This does not account for Retweeting articles or responding to followers.

WEEK OF JANUARY 4:
- Need some books for this month? Find our book reviews here and sign up for our newsletter http://bit.ly/6h9LyM <COMPLETE>
- Are your kids back to school and in need of some homework help? Did you know they can chat live with a librarian? http://bit.ly/8TXbqn - COMPLETE
- In 2009, we had 3 million visitors to our libraries
- It's time for "Who Knew?" Wednesday. Q: How much snow equals an inch of rain? <COMPLETE>
- Who Knew A: On average, 13 inches of snow is translated as 1 inch of rain. <COMPLETE>
- Join us for a free family-friendly concert on Sunday, January 10 from 2 to 2:30 p.m. at Main Library. <link> COMPLETE
- Last year, customers borrowed more than 16 million items, made 8.2 million visits to the library and asked 1.2 million reference questions. COMPLETE
- January is National Thank You month and we want to honor the thousands of volunteers who allow us to provide an invaluable service to the community. Without them, it wouldn't be possible.

WEEK OF JANUARY 11:
- Great book reviews from The Columbus Dispatch http://bit.ly/8jDT5R
- Who Knew Wednesday – Q: Why is corned beef called "corned" when it doesn't have anything to do with corn?
- Who Knew Wednesday – A: There are two definitions for "corned". 1. Formed into grains. 2. Of meat; preserved or cured with salt
- Most popular books of 2009 were: _____
- Most anticipated books for 2010 are:_____
- Winners of CML Scriptwriting Contest
- In honor of Ben Franklin's birthday, check out this biography. (January 17) – include a link to a book

---

FIGURE 4.2 **Twitter content calendar for Columbus Metropolitan Library. Courtesy of the Columbus Metropolitan Library, Columbus, Ohio.**

WEEK OF JANUARY 18:
- In observance of Martin Luther King Jr. Day, the library will be closed.
- Our favorite books on Martin Luther King Jr. are <link>
- Any stats about Martin Luther King Jr. and Ohio?
- Who Knew Wednesday – Q:
- Who Knew Wednesday – A:
- Need some book suggestions for teens? Try these http://bit.ly/8P2Alg COMPLETE
- We've just opened our 18th Homework Help Center at Main Library <link to release or photo> COMPLETE

WEEK OF JANUARY 25:
- We just launched two new blogs "Great Reads" and "All History is Local" <link to general blogs>
- Check out the latest post on…… <link to blog>
- Who Knew Wednesday – Q:
- Who Knew Wednesday – A:
- Looking for some eBooks or audiobooks? Try this site http://bit.ly/3ErNEO COMPLETE
- Did you know we're on Facebook? Find us here http://bit.ly/7gm67A COMPLETE

WEEK OF FEBRUARY 1:
- In honor of Black History month, we'll provide an interesting perspective from our community each week throughout February. COMPLETE
- Facts about Black History – in Columbus, highlight historic black community members - COMPLETE
- Happy Groundhog Day, Happy Groundhog Day
- Have a question, ask our experts – chat live, call or e-mail. We give Google a run for its money. http://bit.ly/Te546
- Our bookmobile is visiting XX (number) of senior living communities this week to deliver free books. Statistic (how many books did we provide last year?) <include a photo>
- Blog post link
- Who Knew Wednesday – Q:
- Who Knew Wednesday – A:

WEEK OF FEBRUARY 8:
- *Facts about Black History – in Columbus, highlight historic black community members*

cont.

- Today is Boy Scout Day, did you know that the library offers troops
  …..
- Blog post link
- Who Knew Wednesday – Q:
- Who Knew Wednesday – A:
- Are you ready for Valentine's Day? Need to make a romantic dinner or a decadent dessert - check out these books for a little help. <provide a link>
- Perfect gift for a book lover – a library card (it's free and thoughtful).
- History of Valentine's Day – link to a post explaining its significance

WEEK OF FEBRUARY 15:
- Happy President's Day. The library will be closed today.
- Interesting facts about presidents from Ohio
- Facts about Black History – in Columbus, highlight historic black community members
- Blog post link
- Who Knew Wednesday – Q:
- Who Knew Wednesday – A:

WEEK OF FEBRUARY 22:
- *Facts about Black History – in Columbus, highlight historic black community members*
- Blog post link
- Who Knew Wednesday – Q:
- Who Knew Wednesday – A:
- Ready 2 Read Corps is making its way through central Ohio communities to help parents and caregivers teach kids how to read thanks to donations from _____. <link to article and photo>
- There are six reading skills children need to know before kindergarten and our Ready 2 Read team is getting them ready.
- Our goal is to increase kindergarten readiness to 90 percent or higher.
- Six reading skills needed for kindergarteners – storytelling, ABCs, sound, loving books, words and using books. More information here <include a link>

FIGURE 4.2 **(cont.)**

FACEBOOK CONTENT CALENDAR

The following items are suggestions for content development for each week. This is a flexible document so if something needs to be changed or moved to a different date that is not a problem. This provides us with a starting point in order to develop and create some possible topics for discussion.

WEEK OF JANUARY 4:
- Looking for a few good books to read this month? Check out our book reviews and sign up for our Great Reads newsletter. http://bit.ly/6h9LyM <COMPLETE>
- Are your kids back to school and in need of some homework help? Did you know they can chat live with a librarian to get answers to their questions? http://kids.columbuslibrary.org/ebranch/index.cfm?pageid=248
- Does your child need some additional one-on-one tutoring? Check out one of our Homework Help Centers. <link>
- We're starting a new feature every week called "Who Knew?" Wednesday. This week's question is – How much snow equals an inch of rain? A: On average, 13 inches of snow is translated as 1 inch of rain. <COMPLETE>
- We're offering a free family-friendly concert. Join us for Music by the Numbers on Sunday, January 10 from 2 to 2:30 p.m. at Main Library. ProMusica brass quintet will be performing. <link> <COMPLETE>
- January is National Thank You month and we want to honor the thousands of volunteers who allow us to provide an invaluable service to the community. Without them, it wouldn't be possible.

WEEK OF JANUARY 11:
- Upload photos of the Music by the Numbers event
- We've compiled a list of the most popular books of 2009. They include:____. What was your favorite book of 2009? Join our discussion.
- Who Knew Wednesday – Q: Why is corned beef called "corned" when it doesn't have anything to do with corn? A: There are two definitions for "corned". 1. Formed into grains. 2. Of meat; preserved or cured with salt.

cont.

FIGURE 4.3 **Facebook content calendar for Columbus Metropolitan Library. Courtesy of the Columbus Metropolitan Library, Columbus, Ohio.**

- Discussion: What books are you looking forward to reading in 2010?
- Winners of CML Scriptwriting Contest
- In honor of Ben Franklin's birthday, check out this biography. (January 17) – include a link to a book

WEEK OF JANUARY 18:
- Today is Martin Luther King Jr. Day. The library will be closed in observance of this day.
- Our favorite books on Martin Luther King Jr. are <link>
- Any stats about Martin Luther King Jr. and Ohio?
- Who Knew Wednesday – Q: Who Knew Wednesday – A:
- Reserves on the rise include *Altar of Eden*, by James Rollins; *Olive Kitteridge*, by Elizabeth Strout; *How We Decide*, by Jonah Lehrer; *The Guinea Pig Diaries*, by A. J. Jacobs; and *Day After Night*, by Anita Diamant
- Need some book suggestions for teens? Try these http://bit.ly/dcb-jUK
- We've just opened our 18th Homework Help Center at Main Library, 96 S. Grant Ave. and are looking forward to helping students in the community. <include link and upload a photo album> The final three Homework Help Centers will be completed in 2010.

WEEK OF JANUARY 25:
- We just launched two new blogs "Great Reads" and "All History is Local" <link to general blogs>
- Who Knew Wednesday – Q: Who Knew Wednesday – A:
- Our bookmobile is visiting XX (number) of senior living communities this week to deliver free books. Statistic (how many books did we provide last year?) – include a photo.
- Did you know we're on Twitter too? Find and follow us here <link>

WEEK OF FEBRUARY 1:
- In honor of Black History month, we'll provide an interesting perspective from our community. We'll start every week with an interesting fact, figure or member of our community who made a contribution. *Facts about Black History – in Columbus, highlight historic black community members*
- Blog post link
- Who Knew Wednesday – Q: Who Knew Wednesday – A:

FIGURE 4.3 **(cont.)**

WEEK OF FEBRUARY 8:

- *Facts about Black History – in Columbus, highlight historic black community members*
- Blog post link
- Who Knew Wednesday – Q: Who Knew Wednesday – A:
- Are you ready for Valentine's Day? Need to make a romantic dinner or a decadent dessert - check out these books for a little help. <provide a link>

WEEK OF FEBRUARY 15:

- Happy President's Day. The library will be closed today.
- Interesting facts about presidents from Ohio
- *Facts about Black History – in Columbus, highlight historic black community members*
- Blog post link
- Who Knew Wednesday – Q: Who Knew Wednesday – A:

WEEK OF FEBRUARY 22:

- *Facts about Black History – in Columbus, highlight historic black community members*
- Blog post link
- Who Knew Wednesday – Q: Who Knew Wednesday – A:
- Ready 2 Read Corps is making its way through central Ohio communities to help parents and caregivers teach kids how to read thanks to donations from _____. Our goal is to increase kindergarten readiness to 90 percent or higher. <link to article and photo>
- There are six reading skills children need to know before kindergarten and our Ready 2 Read team is getting them ready. Six reading skills needed for kindergarteners – storytelling, ABCs, sound, loving books, words and using books. More information here <include a link>

RETHINKING
STATUS UPDATES

You need to clean out those old sources of your social-media diet that are no longer nourishing, dust the cobwebs off those old connections to keep them polished and valuable, and clean out the dirt from the corners of your social life where you haven't ventured in months.

—ERIC FULWILER[1]

Social media is an ephemeral medium. Your post may catch the attention of someone only for as long as they are actually looking at it. They will quickly move on to other content, especially if your update is lacking in some way. I often receive questions from library staff about how to make updates more interesting or relevant to the end user. In chapter 4, we examined some specific status updates and examples of how they could be made better. In this section, we will take a closer look, examining additional and common problems with library status updates, and more models for effective engagement.

MISTAKE: NOT MAKING IT EASY

The nature of social media often makes people somewhat lazy: it presents a stream of instant information in real or almost-real time. That stream comes directly to the reader in most cases, and does not involve much, if any, effort to obtain. Arguably, people are becoming used to having information pushed to them, rather than having to retrieve it. One result of this is that readers of your content are becoming less likely to make the effort to get additional information about what you're posting—unless they're very motivated to do so. Take this status update:

Check out our hottest summer DVD releases!

This post does not even include a link that would potentially make it easy to find out what new releases a library has. A patron is very unlikely to come to the library and say, "I saw your post about the hot new summer DVDs. Where are they?" She'll want to know what the actual titles are before ever physically going to the library and, if possible, may want to reserve them in advance. Unfortunately, neither action is possible in this case; no information was provided to allow her to do so.

A similar problem occurs with this update:

Read Dan Porat's The Boy: A Holocaust
Story. To be ordered on 11/21.

Here, the post tells the reader to carry out an action (reading a particular book), but there isn't a link allowing one to learn more about the book or reserve it. Chances are good that once this tweet is out of sight, it will also be out of mind for the reader. If the library wanted more people to read this book as a result of the post, it's very likely it failed to do so.

In both cases, each post could be made significantly more effective simply by the addition of a hyperlink to relevant information. Even on Facebook and some other networks, where there is a much higher character limit on posts, it's always a good idea to include a link to the more permanent home of the information on your library's website. This not only prevents readers from becoming overwhelmed by too much text, but it can also help to increase your site's incoming traffic. If your website metrics show referrers (where people came from to get to your site), this can also provide another way for you to gauge the potential impact of your social media posts.

Some updates may simply be missing important information. Think about this library's tweet:

Today at 3:45, we are showing a new release
on our BIG projector screen! Hope to see
you there. Free, no need to register.

This post mentions the date and time and even the fact that registration is not required. Yet it is missing what many might consider the most important piece of information anyone would want: the movie's title! How many people are going to want to take the time to figure out the library's phone number and call the library just to get this information?

Missing information may also be based on an assumption that the reader already has it. This library's post seems to make such an assumption:

> *Author Rob Smith is coming to the*
> *library tonight at 7 pm.*

The problem here is, if one's not familiar with the author, there's no incentive to attend the program. Also, as with earlier examples, there's no link to more information. A remade post might look something like this:

> *Local author Rob Smith (http://smithwrite.*
> *net), author of the McGowan Chronicles, will*
> *be speaking here tonight at 7 pm [LINK].*

At the very least, this provides a little bit of context for the readers who are not aware of the author's work.

Present the most interesting information in the social media post and include a link to more information. The first two previous examples could be remade to look something like these:

> *Hot new summer DVD releases are here. Reserve*
> *them while they're…well…hot: [LINK].*

> *Get in line to be one of the first to get Dan*
> *Porat's The Boy: A Holocaust Story [LINK].*

Both of these remade examples not only link to more information, but they may also give the reader a sense of urgency that might make him or her more likely to take the action being recommended.

BOTTOM LINE ▸ Don't make your library's fans or followers work to get what you want them to know or do. Include essential information. Make the post interesting enough to hook them and (hopefully) entice them into taking further action with a provided link.

MISTAKE: NOT MAKING THE PAYOFF CLEAR

Libraries often give at least the appearance of assuming people will just naturally want to come to their programs or take advantage of their services. Consider this post:

> *Mango Languages is a new online resource*
> *available to users of all public libraries in our*
> *state. It includes a variety . . . [LINK].*

It's probably at least a bit exciting to the library staff that this new resource is available to the public, but there is no real sense of this enthusiasm being communicated in this update. Further hindering engagement is that there's nothing in this post to hook possible users to try the new resource. What the reader might get from Mango Languages is not stated at all. Compare that to this remade version:

> *Learn a new language. Today. For free.*
> *Online. With your library card. Introducing*
> *Mango Languages: [LINK].*

The difference is plain: the second version tells readers exactly what they are going to get before the library even mentions the name of the product. The remade message also gives the information that is most likely to hook a user: the library says right up front that the reader can learn a new language for free and online with just a library card. By doing these things it's much more effective; it prioritizes the needs of the end user over the thing being promoted.

Libraries sometimes also produce updates that may seem irrelevant to non–library staff. Take this example:

> *National Library Week, April 10–16. [LINK]*

If readers are not aware of National Library Week, there is nothing to hook them. Even if readers *are* aware of National Library Week, is there any real incentive to learn more? Simply knowing the subject matter of a post is not usually enough to drive someone to take any action on it. In this case, the library would be better off promoting a series of special events, or asking followers to help the library celebrate in a particular way that sounds interesting to the reader.

BOTTOM LINE ▶ Always remember that posts have to be written as to be relevant to the reader immediately. If readers can't quickly figure out what's in it for them, the post will be judged irrelevant and will be ignored.

MISTAKE: BEING TOO BOSSY

Give some thought to the following status updates. Can you spot the common issue with all of them?

Come to "Local Herbalist Shares History of Herbal Medicines" today from 7:00 pm to 9:00 pm. [LINK]

Check out Second National Bank's window on Main Street for this fantastic display put up by staff. [LINK]

Come to "Library Seeks Candidate for Trustee Position" today from 6:30 pm to 9:30 pm. [LINK]

Join our new Book Discussion Group! [LINK]

Be a member of our new Patron Advisory Board. [LINK]

Try our new research database for your next assignment. [LINK]

All of these updates, and many others produced by libraries, begin with command words. Words such as *come, check out, join,* and *be* all tell the user to do something, rather than ask for a response. The problem is compounded because not only is the library in each post commanding the reader to perform an action, but there is also no apparent reason for the reader to comply. Where's the payoff? If your library chooses to take a carrot-and-stick approach to social media, it must at least remember to provide the carrot.

Each of the prior examples could be made over like this:

Curious about the history of herbal medicines?
Local herbalist tells all beginning at 7 pm. [LINK]

It took 2 hours, 4 staff and more than 500
yards of streamers. What do you think of the
display we did for Second National Bank
on Main Street? [LINK TO PHOTO]

Not everyone is cut out to be a Library Trustee—are
you? We're looking for a new one for next year. [LINK]

Can't stop talking about that book you just read?
Yeah, us too. Now we've got a group for that: [LINK]

Looking for opinionated folks who want to talk
about the library. Cookies at every meeting
and a chance to make a difference. [LINK]

Wikipedia not good enough for your
teacher? Show 'em you're a smart cookie
and try a free resource from us. [LINK]

BOTTOM LINE Avoid sounding like a drill sergeant by not issuing updates that command readers to do something. If you can't avoid commands, at least be sure to make it clear what the reader will get by following the command.

MISTAKE: BEING OVERLY EXCITED

If you were to look at a collection of social media posts gathered from an assortment of libraries, you might begin to notice a trend concerning the use of exclamation points. Many, many status updates use exclamation points as if adding them to a piece of social media content will somehow make it inherently more exciting and urgent. Take, for example:

Remember that your library's patrons are inundated with requests and demands. Don't let your social media updates add to their feelings of being overwhelmed.

Harry Potter Party at the Main Library
Thursday, July 14, at 3 pm!!!!!!!!

Adding more than one exclamation point is intended to convey extreme excitement. But what about the following?

BEAT THE HEAT! CAN'T GO TO THE
POOL? KEEP COOL AT YOUR LIBRARY!

Please take our brief survey! [LINK]

Library has reopened! Check out our new
carpet, brighter lighting and more! [LINK]

Crafts and Fun around the World! Grades K–4,
Thursday, 10:30–11:30 am! Registration required,
Call [PHONE NUMBER] for more information!

Don't forget to register for the Princess
Party this Friday! [LINK]

Some of these status updates exhibit other problems as well, but they all have unnecessary exclamation points in common.

Exclamation points, by nature, indicate that something is (significantly) more important than something else. They're used to indicate emphasis for a particular thing. When they are used constantly, it quickly diminishes their meaning and effectiveness, much like crying "Wolf!" constantly. James Chartrand, a copywriter and founder of the online community Men with Pens, writes:

> There are the exclamation-point addicts out there, you see. They're the writers who feel they really can't put across the excitement, immediacy, or sincerity without that little extra boost (!) to make it feel super-charged. They're the writers who believe that they should slap an exclamation point at the end of a written sentence anytime they would allow their voice to lift at the end of spoken one. . . . Exclamation points, you see, are evil.[2]

Chartrand says that using them can make the reader doubt the authenticity of the statement. "If you have confidence in what you say, in what you write, you sound much more believable without exclamation points. Every time. No exceptions."[3]

Social media offers a much less formal communications platform than many, yet being able to write effectively is just as important. Professional writers rarely, if ever, use exclamation points in their writing. If you examine the social media updates of major companies or institutions, you'll usually be hard-put to find any, let alone a constant stream of them. Here are some tweets from well-known entities:

Really great feedback from #blogchat participants
tonight. Awesome discussion re customer
service via blogs, social media, etc. (Dell)

*From 2006 to 2010, Harvard spawned 39 start-
up companies, 216 patents, and 1,270 faculty
inventions. #numberswednesday (Harvard University)*

*Be careful in the heat this week. Stay cool (and
classy) with these tips: [LINK] (American Red Cross)*

*Enjoying your Morning Joe? Find out
how coffee experts crown Colombia's
best beans. [LINK] (Wired magazine)*

*More than 1000 languages spoken in New Guinea.
One of the most culturally and biological diverse
places on earth. [LINK] (Smithsonian Education)*

Try replacing the periods in each of these with an exclamation point. Chances are, the results will make you cringe.

BOTTOM LINE ▸ Exclamation points do not make your library's content more exciting. Rather, they increase the likelihood of it looking unprofessional, causing the reader to doubt its sincerity. Focus on writing interesting updates that do not use exclamation points as a crutch.

MISTAKE: AUTOMATED CONTENT

There are many apps that allow one to automatically post content from other sites to one's social network accounts. For example, you may be familiar with tweets such as this one:

*I posted 6 photos on Facebook in the album
"Cool Crafts 2011." [LINK]*

There's a lot to be said for the convenience of having an application automatically announce new content. However, this kind of update will usually be ignored. There's no payoff for the reader and, more important, it's plain to see that it *is* automated, especially since the format of these types of items doesn't change significantly. There's simply no attempt to engage the reader: this post and its ilk make a simple announcement that's almost certain to be discounted by the library's followers. Some people even consider these kinds of updates to be spam.

Rather than waste effort (and turn off your library's fans in the process), make sure to add some relevant context to posted content. Simply announcing new content may not be enough to garner any real interest. Find the hook, or the payoff, that is going to make the content interesting enough for someone to want to click the link and actually see it. Try something like this:

> *Geodomes made with gumdrops, constructed*
> *with care by our local kids. See the pics: [LINK]*

Being specific here has value; the announcement is not generic. The craft idea may be unique to some, and by stating that local children are involved it may inspire some to click the link to see if they know the kids.

It should be noted there's a difference between automating the content of posts and automating their actual posting to a social network. There are many ways to schedule updates at future times, such as using social media dashboards like Tweetdeck or Hootsuite, or many third-party applications specifically developed to publish social media content on specific dates and times. These tools can be very helpful in spreading the social media workload evenly. Just remember the content that is scheduled still needs to be engaging.

BOTTOM LINE ▶ Scheduling your content for automatic publishing is fine, but beware of apps that publish announcements that end up being worthless or annoying to the library's fans or followers.

MISTAKE: FORCING FANS AND FOLLOWERS TO ANOTHER MEDIUM OR NETWORK

Consider this question, posted by a mother to a library's Facebook Wall:

> *I'd like to bring my daughter to your storytime.*
> *What day and time is it held?*

Then ponder the library's response:

We offer storytime several times a week,
for different age groups. Please call
the library at [PHONE NUMBER].

The problem with the library's response may not be obvious, unless you are the mother who asked the question of the library. The original poster asked the question in one medium—Facebook—and instead of being answered in that medium, she was told to switch to another: the telephone. It's likely that this woman felt considerable frustration after receiving this response. She may have thought she could get a quick, easy answer from asking the question on Facebook, rather than having to potentially wade through a telephone system to get the information she needed. Instead of inadvertently making this harder for the mother, the library could have handled this two different ways, depending on the circumstances:

- The library could have linked directly to its storytime schedule on its website (assuming that there was such a schedule there).
- The library could have responded with a question of its own, asking for additional information from the mother. Knowing what age the daughter is would allow the library to quickly answer the question. If privacy is a concern, the mother could privately message the information to the library's Facebook Page administrator via Facebook's messaging system.

Occasionally, a library will try to get patrons to jump from one network to another in order to obtain content. One example is this library's tweet:

Click "Like" on our Facebook Page to see
all of our cool programs. [LINK]

If someone is following the library on Twitter, they will probably expect this content to be available via either tweets or possibly through links to the library's website. Forcing someone to become a fan of the library on another network will turn at least some followers off. It's hardly fair to expect someone to click "Like" just to get what should be rightfully available in other places of the medium (or another medium) that person is already engaged in with the library.

BOTTOM LINE ➤ Make every effort to respond to queries in the same medium in which they're made. Don't turn off your library's supporters, or potential ones, by forcing them to jump through hoops to get content.

MISTAKE: NOT GETTING TO THE POINT

Since it has a limit of only 140 characters, Twitter forces content writers to create very succinct updates. Nevertheless, some libraries attempt to bypass the limit by linking to what amounts to the rest of a tweet. For example:

> *Margaret Mitchell's Gone with the Wind, one of the best-selling novels of all time and the basis for an Academy Award winning film… [LINK]*

This post is making an assumption: that the reader will bother to click and read the rest of it. Considering that people's tweet streams may have hundreds of messages per hour, the chances of someone bothering to click a link, just to read the rest of this statement, are very low. This issue is closely related to the problem of not having an immediate and clear payoff for the reader. Here's one with a similar concern:

> *During the Great Depression, not one single public library closed its doors. See this amazing… [LINK]*

This statement is even more vague than the first example, since it's completely left to the reader to guess the point of the post. While the mystery may intrigue some people, the majority will ignore it. Hoping to interest readers by intentionally leaving off details is unlikely to be a successful ploy: Twitter followers are quickly scanning their streams, looking for pertinent information. If you can't provide something that proves itself immediately relevant to them, the content will be passed over. Worse, repeated irrelevance and vague tweets may lead to a library being unfollowed (we'll examine this more in just a moment).

If you can't make the point clear and the reward obvious in 140 characters, it may be that the content is better suited for a social network such as Facebook, where the text limit is much higher. Bear in mind tweets that take up all or nearly all of the available characters have an additional hitch: they cannot be easily retweeted by others, since they will need to attribute the tweet to your library and that will require more characters. "As a general rule, if you want your tweet to be easily retweetable, make it no more than 120 characters including the link,"[4] says Yvette Pistorio, the Social Media Community Manager at Cision.

BOTTOM LINE ▶ Never assume anyone will keep reading your library's content if they have to go somewhere else to get the rest of it. Be relevant, immediately, or be ignored.

MISTAKE: FLOODING OTHERS WITH UPDATES

Recently, I felt forced to unfollow some libraries on Twitter. I could always tell when their appointed people would sit down in the mornings to do their social media work, because my Twitter stream would immediately be filled with many consecutive (usually banal) tweets, announcing programs or events. Here's a sample from one such library; all of these came in consecutively, literally within one minute:

> *Tiddlywinks! When: Wednesday, July 13, 2011— 10:00 am. Where: Children's Area at Main. [LINK]*

> *Poolside Stories @ Community Pool: When: Wednesday, July 13, 2011—2:00 pm. [LINK]*

> *Poolside @ the Civic Center: When: Wednesday, July 27, 2011—2:00 pm. [LINK]*

> *Storytime @ Public Pool: When: Wednesday, July 13, 2011—2:00.*

> *Chess Club for Kids: When: Wednesday, July 27, 2011—2:30. [LINK]*

Five posts within a minute are far too many, too fast. Essentially, I felt that these libraries were spamming me on a daily basis. Mike Johansson, a social media strategist and visiting professor in the department of communication at the Rochester Institute of Technology, says that this is one of the ten most common newbie Twitter mistakes. "If you're guilty of this you will annoy your followers and water down your message . . . which likely means you'll lose followers faster than you get them."[5] As tempting as it might be to get all of your content out there at once, this method will not support your library's social media efforts.

Fine-tuning your library's quantity of posts is important. Johansson recommends starting slowly, posting only two or three times per day. As your library works toward increasing this amount, pay attention to what actually garners responses or engagement, such as comments or retweets. Use these examples as your guideposts for what works and what doesn't. Another way to spread the work out is to use one of the many tools that can automate social media posting. By scheduling updates to be published at future times, your library can ensure it's not inadvertently spamming any of its followers.

BOTTOM LINE   Spread posts out and don't deluge fans or followers with too much content at once. Small, digestible, and occasional bites are far preferable and are less likely to alienate people permanently.

NOTES

1. Eric Fulwiler, "An 8-Step Plan for Social Media Spring Cleaning," April 1, 2010, www .blog.ericfulwiler.com/social-media/an-8-step-plan-for-social-media-spring-cleaning.

2. James Chartrand, "Is Your Website Copy Too Excited?" *Men with Pens*, 2009, http:// menwithpens.ca/no-exclamation-points.

3. Ibid.

4. Yvette Pistorio, "5 Twitter Mistakes to Avoid," June 30, 2011, http://blog.us.cision .com/2011/06/5-twitter-mistakes-to-avoid.

5. Mike Johansson, "10 Newbie Twitter Mistakes Made By Businesses," *Social Media Today*, March 8, 2010, http://socialmediatoday.com/index.php?q=SMC/179967.

6

FINE-TUNING FACEBOOK

Like print newspapers, basketball players under 6 feet tall, and the McRib sandwich, the website as we know it will soon be a thing of the past—a quaint reminder of the original Internet era. Who killed the website? Facebook, of course.

—JAY BAER, OF CONVINCE & CONVERT

Will Facebook kill websites as we know them? It's likely too early to predict the death of websites at the hands of a particular brand of social media. However, as of this writing, there is no question that Facebook is the undisputed king of social networks. When your library chooses which social tool(s) it will focus on, the chances are high that Facebook will rank near or at the top of its list. If Facebook isn't on your library's short list, it almost certainly should be. Consider these statistics:

- In 2011, 70 percent of small business owners chose to use Facebook for marketing their products or services; that's up from 50 percent in 2010.[1]
- Facebook has more than 500 million active users.[2] If Facebook were a country, it would be the third most populous, behind only India and China.[3]
- Of those users, more than 50 percent log on to Facebook on any given day.[4]

- The average Facebook user is connected to eighty Community Pages, groups, and events on the site.[5]
- Facebook's users spend more than 11.67 billion hours per month on the network.[6]

For many libraries, the decision to use Facebook, or at least have a presence on it, is a no-brainer. What takes more thought is how to use it so that there is some objective result. As discussed in earlier chapters, libraries will often, in a reflexive effort to adapt, obtain a social media account, then realize they don't truly understand what to do with it or how to maintain it well. Since Facebook is so prevalent, these kinds of dilemmas present themselves frequently to libraries that involve themselves with social media.

In addition, libraries can easily be intimidated by the frequency of changes to the Facebook interface. Historically, libraries are about permanence and preservation, and almost everything about social media is contrary to what libraries have been founded upon. The fact that Facebook often rearranges and changes its look and functionality can throw less adaptable librarians for a loop. Nonetheless, most libraries have stuck with Facebook and recognized they are potentially building on a foundation made of sand. (Before this book is even published, it's likely some of the information contained in this chapter will become obsolete.) Author Cory Doctorow has pointed out that these constant shifts by Facebook and other social media sites constitute a *feature,* not a bug: "The technology that underpins social media is changing fast, and social media companies' bone-deep intuitions about what it should and shouldn't do are made obsolete every 18 months or so. . . . Only lazy, fat media execs from firms that endured for decades without having to

Figuring out how to make Facebook work to your library's advantage is an ongoing process and will take work.

remake themselves from top to bottom think that a complete turnover in the corporate landscape is a failure."[7] The ability of Facebook to make comprehensive changes (often with short or little notice) is often seen as disconcerting, but it should not be discouraging. Change is rarely comfortable for the end user. Rather, it is a clear indicator that Facebook is working to remain relevant.

Facebook's array of options can also be overwhelming. Should a library have a profile? A Community Page? A group? Is it worthwhile to customize the landing page? Should the library use any of the available built-in applications (apps)? What kinds of posts actually work to get responses on this network?

Facebook can present a library with many questions that can be difficult to find clear answers to, but by committing to regularly engaging these questions, libraries can develop the skills and mind-set to retain relevance and remain connected. What follows are ways not only to answer these questions but also to help your library better use what is at this time the world's largest social network. Think of accepting the challenge to do this as parallel to what a runner experiences from not just surviving a marathon but coming out stronger: they have learned to love running.

BOTTOM LINE ▶ Facebook can be overwhelming, but it is the social media site that most libraries will use the most. Be prepared to (constantly) adapt as Facebook continues to grow.

PROFILES VERSUS PAGES VERSUS BUSINESS ACCOUNTS VERSUS COMMUNITY PAGES

Up until fairly recently, Facebook did not offer libraries, businesses, or other organizations the ability to represent themselves as anything other than an individual. When a library would create an account, it would have to fill in inapplicable information, such as picking a gender. In 2007, Facebook made specific types of accounts available to companies and organizations. This allowed them to more accurately represent themselves, and also included new functionality that only such new accounts could take advantage of. Facebook also changed its terms of service, so that nonindividuals could no longer have regular profiles. Many libraries, if they set up a Facebook profile prior to 2007, may not even be aware they are now in violation of Facebook's rules and are subject to having their accounts shut down entirely. Even if they realize their predicament, they may not know how to switch over or what the differences are between a profile and a page.

To make things even more confusing, Facebook also introduced what it calls "business accounts" and "Community Pages." What are these, and who are they for?

In point of fact, Facebook actually only recognizes two kinds of accounts: personal profiles and organizational Pages. However, there is a subtype of the personal profile called a "business account." Here is Facebook's official take on these:

> Business accounts are designed for individuals who only want to use the site to administer Pages and their ad campaigns. For this reason, business accounts do not have the same functionality as personal accounts. Business accounts have limited access to information on the site. An individual with a business account can view all the Pages and Facebook Ads that they have created, however they will not be able to view the profiles of users on the site or other content on the site that does not live on the Pages they administer. In addition, business accounts cannot be found in search and cannot send or receive friend requests.[8]

In reality, a business account on Facebook is simply a very limited version of a personal profile that someone can set up in order to administer an existing page. This kind of account is largely useless for libraries, since it is a type of personal profile, which libraries (not being individuals) can't use. If your library is considering having someone on staff create a business account to administer the library's Facebook Page, this can quickly become an issue that will put your library in violation of Facebook's terms of service. If the designated staff member already has a Facebook account, or wishes to create a personal profile at a later time, he or she can't. Facebook's rules clearly state that having more than one profile is an offense that can result in the account(s) being deleted.

What about Community Pages? How are they different from a regular Facebook Page? Community Pages are dedicated to a topic or experience, rather than to a locale, business, or organization. Essentially, it is a place on Facebook for like-minded people to interact around a broad subject. Curt Hopkins, writing for ReadWriteWeb, points out that "Unlike a Facebook page devoted to, or run by, a company, a Community Page might be devoted to an area or an activity that cannot be legitimately claimed by a limited group such as a corporation."[9] Although users are welcome to create their own Community Pages, in point of fact, many are auto-created by Facebook directly from raw Wikipedia data. Your library may actually have a Community Page already, but remember that such an auto-created page will not give your library any control and is simply information copied from Wikipedia.

In short, a library cannot maintain a Facebook profile, and it is an unreasonable expectation to imagine a library can control (or therefore effectively use) a Community Page. When it comes to Facebook, libraries only have one legitimate and useful choice: a regular page. While it is possible for a library staff member to maintain that page using a business account, it is likely that in the long term such a strategy will become problematic.

The good news is that Facebook Pages have several unique features that profiles do not have. While a page can't have friends, it does allow people to "like" the library. This is actually an advantage, especially for larger libraries: Facebook's profiles have an upper limit of 5,000 friends, while an unlimited number of people can "like" a page. Pages also come with Facebook's built-in analytics package, Facebook Insights. With Insights, you can gain all kinds of useful data about how your page is used, including demographic breakdowns and measuring which posts get the most reactions. This data is not included with personal profiles. Pages also allow for all sorts of promotion outside of Facebook, with widgets and plug-ins that can easily be embedded in your library's website.

BOTTOM LINE Libraries should be using Facebook Pages. Using personal profiles is in direct violation of Facebook's terms of service; currently other options are either not as robust or may cause other issues down the road.

CONVERTING FROM A PROFILE TO A FACEBOOK PAGE: THE AUTOMATED METHOD

Chances are good that your library may be among the many that created a Facebook profile back in the days before the advent of Facebook Pages. If that's the case, your library now faces the challenge of converting the profile to a page. Facebook does have an automated tool to make this conversion (www .facebook.com/pages/create.php?migrate), although it has been known to be somewhat buggy. There are also some caveats that any library should be aware of before it chooses this method of conversion:

- Any friends the profile had will automatically become people who "like" the new page. This may bewilder your library's Facebook friends if they do not have advance notice. People may otherwise wonder why the library suddenly unfriended them.
- Profile pictures will be transferred over, but *no* other content will be. Keep in mind that you will be starting from scratch. (Even with the manual method, you will need to move content yourself—the only difference is that the automated method will pull your profile pictures.) If you had any photos, videos, or other specialized posts, they will need to be moved manually.
- After the page is created, the original profile will be automatically converted to a business account. This creates two issues: (1) the library is automatically still in violation of Facebook's terms of service, since an organization cannot have any kind of profile, and (2) this account becomes the sole administering account for the newly created page.

Before your library chooses the automated method, be sure to figure out who the new page's administrator is going to be. This will need to be the personal (profile) account of at least one staff member. More than one would be ideal, so that at least several staff members have access in case others are not available. Some libraries may have issues with giving individuals control over the library's Facebook presence. Unfortunately, at this time, it's the only legitimate method of administration available. Once those additional administrators have been assigned, you will need to delete the old profile-now-business-account in order to comply with Facebook's rules.

BOTTOM LINE ▶ The automated method of converting a Facebook profile to a page doesn't convert all of your library's existing content, but it will convert all existing friends to "likes" of the page. However, the hasty way in which it does this may be confusing for the library's friends and still results in a Facebook account that will need to be deleted in the end.

CONVERTING FROM A PROFILE TO A FACEBOOK PAGE: THE MANUAL METHOD

Your library may want to choose the manual method, especially if it wants to be able to give its Facebook friends more warning about the upcoming changes. It's also a good way to bring your library's presence on Facebook to their attention. Here's how to manage the switchover manually.

Step 1: Create the New Page

You will need to start by first creating the new page. This should be done from the personal profile that will be managing the page (see the previous section for more information about personal profiles and administrators). Typically, new pages can be created by going to www.facebook.com/pages/create.php, once you are logged into Facebook. Be sure to be as complete as possible when filling out the information fields offered. Remember, profiles matter—people will judge whether or not to "like" your library's page based on the information available. The goal is to have any new connections "like" the newly created page, while working toward weaning existing connections away from the old profile.

Step 2: Camouflage the Old Profile

The point of Facebook is to connect with others, so while it's not possible to hide the old profile away (so that new people cannot friend it) you can scale back the privacy settings of the old profile so it's not so easy to find. The profile likely allows "everyone" to see it and its content. Change any privacy setting that allows for "Friends only" to that option. This will make the profile less appealing. It also means that anyone who wants to see the content who is not already a friend of the library's profile will need to make a friend request. When the library receives such a request, it can reply with the address of the library's new page and briefly explain that it is in the process of transition from a profile to a page.

Step 3: Set a (Public) Deadline

John Paul Titlow, a writer for ReadWriteWeb, says: "The process of converting a profile to a page is very time-sensitive. You want to be quick about it, but not so fast that you fail to get the attention of your existing friends and end up losing those connections without an explanation."[10] While Titlow recommends about two weeks' notice, this amount of time may not be entirely practical in the case of notifying what may be a much more far-flung community than an individual might have. Plan on at least two weeks, but no longer than a month, before you delete the old profile. Make this deadline very clear and advertise it in many venues (see the next section).

Step 4: Get the Message Out—Often and Quickly

The first place to announce the change is, of course, on the library's original profile. Be sure to give people a direct link to the new page to make it as easy as possible for them to participate. Be emphatic about the date on which the old profile will disappear, and be clear that people will no longer be friends with the library but rather will be able to "like" the new page. Following is a sample message your library could use to advertise the move:

> Unfriend us on Facebook. No, really. We mean it.
>
> You probably don't hear that too often, but we're aiming for a total of zero friends on Facebook.
>
> Why?
>
> When the library's Facebook account was originally set up, it was set up as if it were an individual person, rather than an organization. Back in the day, there wasn't really a good option for organizations, businesses, or other entities to have a page without declaring themselves to be a single person. It wasn't a good fit, and it fits even less well now, since Facebook has added the ability to create pages specifically for organizations.
>
> We're recreating ourselves on Facebook, and we need your help. Start by unfriending us (you won't hurt our feelings, honest!) at our old place: [INSERT OLD PROFILE URL HERE] then go to [INSERT NEW PAGE URL HERE] and click the "Like" button at the top.
>
> Thanks for your help while we work to make this switch by [INSERT DATE HERE].

Be sure to post every day or so, changing the wording so that the messages don't appear automated. Aside from the regular posts to the Facebook profile, include messages on the library's website and on signage at the library in prominent locations. If your library also has a Twitter account, that is a good way to notify people of the change, and it may also draw additional attention to the library's new Facebook presence.

After Completing the Manual Conversion

Following are a few things to remember once you have completed the steps in the manual conversion:

- *Understand that you're not likely to get a 100 percent conversion rate.* This is especially true if your library had a very large number of friends. Some may simply ignore the messages (assuming they even saw them), or they may never go to the trouble to unfriend or click the new page's "Like" button. This is a known side effect of the process, and your library may need to put more effort into gaining new fans after all is said and done.
- *Delete the old profile.* Once you've hit the deadline, it's time to delete the original profile. This can be accomplished by submitting a request for deletion to Facebook at www.facebook.com/help/contact .php?show_form=delete_account. You must be logged in with the original profile account. Deactivating the account is not the same as deletion; deactivating allows for the possibility of using the account at some point in the future. Deactivation is not the option a library should choose, as this is still in violation of Facebook's terms of service.
- *Get a vanity URL.* Once your new page has twenty-five fans or more, you are able to get a custom URL that will be easier to promote and easier for people to remember. Go to www.facebook.com/ username to choose it. Vanity URLs have to be unique; if someone or something else is already using the one you want, you will need to choose a different username/URL. Make sure that you intend to keep it for the long term; pages can only have their usernames changed once—ever.

BOTTOM LINE The manual method of converting a Facebook profile to a page takes longer and does not automatically transfer all of the library's friends to page "likes." However, it may be less confusing for the library's friends. Regardless of which method your library chooses, it will still need to designate the personal profiles of some library staff to administer the new page.

TWEAKING YOUR PAGE

Once your library has a Facebook Page, it's important to take some time to develop and configure it properly. Pages operate somewhat differently from profiles, and include options that your library's profile didn't previously have access to. To take advantage of all of the new features, you'll want to make some changes to the default settings and spend some time working with the new functionality:

- *The Wall filter.* On a page, posts can be filtered to show posts by everyone or only posts by the library. For the best possible engagement, you'll want to be sure that the filter shows all posts, and not just posts by the library's page. Also, it's probably best if the Wall be the default for viewing when people land on the page; while photos and discussions can be interesting, they're not likely to be as interactive or up-to-the-moment as wall posts.
- *E-mail notifications.* A newer feature for Facebook Pages is the ability to get e-mails when someone posts to your page. This is invaluable for helping your library to monitor activity on its wall. You can specify to which e-mail address you'd like such notifications sent.
- *Using Facebook as the page.* With the new pages, you now have the option to post items to the library's page *as* the page, rather than as you, the administrator's personal profile. This can help with keeping authoring and branding consistent. In addition, you can continue to do other things on Facebook, such as "liking" other pages as your library rather than as you as an individual. While this feature is very helpful, it can also cause issues for the unwary. You will need to ensure that you are in the proper setting (human or library) before posting anything on Facebook, if you are a page administrator.
- *Setting your featured "likes."* Your library undoubtedly will want to "like" some other pages, such as neighboring libraries or library-related organizations or local businesses. You can choose which of these to feature on the left side of your page, by going to "Edit Page" and selecting "Featured." You can change or add to these at any time.
- *Showing your page's administrators.* You can also choose which page administrators to feature on the left-hand side of the page, much as you can choose featured "likes." Click "Edit Page" and select "Featured," which will allow you to choose from the list of current page administrators. You can select all or just one or two. Regardless of how

many or which you choose, this is a good idea for any library. Showing who's in charge helps add an element of transparency and credibility.

- *Considering more photos.* Facebook has added some enhancements to its photo functionality that make it even more useful to libraries. You can now upload high resolution photos (up to 2,048 pixels wide or high). Rather than having to first edit images for size before uploading, many libraries will now be able to upload pictures to Facebook from their digital camera directly. Facebook has also added a very nice lightbox interface and removed pagination (all album photos now appear on a single page, where in the past it only allowed twenty photos per page). Overall, these improvements make photos easier to share and more enjoyable for the end user to browse.

- *Claiming your place on Facebook Places.* Facebook Places allows people to "check in" to a real-world location via their laptop, smartphone, or other mobile device. It's a tool that can provide a clear connection between your library's social media presence and its physical one. As of this writing, there is, unfortunately, no clear connection between Facebook Pages and Places. Start by claiming your library's place page on Facebook; place pages are created when someone checks into a venue for the first time. If no one has checked into your library with Facebook Places, you may need to be the first one to do so in order to claim the page that will be created. Then promote it with such tactics as putting signage on your library's doors, encouraging people to check in on their mobile devices with Facebook Places. This encourages people to send out "I am here" messages about the library.

- *Using Facebook Questions.* Just as you can share news, links, photos, and other content with your library's fans, Facebook Pages also allow you to ask a poll question to them as well. When people respond to the poll, their activity shows up in their news feeds, drawing more attention to the library. It's a very good tool for soliciting feedback, but be wary of asking generic, boring questions, such as "Which of the following is your favorite book?" Know what you're going to *do* with the responses; there should be some quantifiable reason for why you ask the question. Don't ask use Facebook Questions simply as a way to do something on the page.

BOTTOM LINE ▶ Facebook Pages have a good number of functions that your library can and should take advantage of. Spend some time investigating these fully so your library can reap the most benefit from its efforts.

WHAT CAN I DO WITH TIMELINE?

Facebook forced the new Timeline format on all Facebook Pages in March 2012. While there is still much controversy and angst from the user community over this change, overall its new features are a boon to libraries looking to really get control over their presence on Facebook. Now, a library's Facebook Wall need not be just a chronological river of postings, because individual posts can be better managed and the new cover photo can better reflect a library's identity and even has some creative uses. What follows is a brief overview of some of the most important features of the new Timeline format.

- *Pinning.* The "Pin to top" option (accessed by clicking the "Edit or remove" pencil icon) allows one to keep a particular post at the top of the Timeline. Even when newer posts are added, posts that are pinned will stay at the top until the "pinned" option is disabled. The post also becomes larger and will extend over both the right and left Timeline columns. Facebook recommends pinning at least one post per week in order to extend the shelf life and interest of your content.
- *Highlighting.* This is very similar to pinning in that the highlighted post will spread across both Timeline columns. However, once newer posts are added to the Timeline, a highlighted post will be pushed down, unlike a pinned post. Highlighting a post will help users to see your best content and separate it out from that which is not as important.
- *Milestones.* A Facebook milestone is essentially a previous event that is added to the Timeline. Examples may include the founding of a library, when a library first became automated, or when a library did a major renovation or moved. Be sure to include these kinds of benchmarks on your library's Timeline. Lauren Drell, the campaigns editor at Mashable.com, says:

  > Milestones add a human touch to your brand and encourage consumers to learn more about your company and thus, become more invested in it. Consumers are curious and love to know more about their favorite brands, and Milestones are a great way to make it easy for them while also eliciting "Likes" and subtly marketing your brand.[11]

- *Cover photo with embedded profile image.* The cover image on a brand page is the large (851×315 pixels) image at the top of the Timeline. A recent eye-tracking study found that people pay more attention to this image than to anything else on a Facebook Page,[12] so the importance of this feature cannot be underestimated. Additionally, a small image is now partially embedded in the cover image—this is the profile image. Most experts agree that the profile image should be the brand or organization's logo, while the cover image should be used more creatively. Some libraries use this space to regularly advertise major programs or events, or to showcase photos of recent happenings in their libraries. It should be noted that Facebook has some strict rules about what kinds of things cannot appear in a cover image. These include:

- o Any contact information, such as a website address, e-mail, mailing address, or information that should go in a page's "About" section
- o References to Facebook actions, such as "Like" or "Share" or an arrow pointing from the cover photo to any of these features
- o Calls to action, such as "Get it now" or "Tell your friends"

BOTTOM LINE ▶ While the Timeline format may take some getting used to, it does provide more advanced functionality for organizing and featuring content.

WHAT ABOUT CUSTOMER LANDING PAGES?

While it is technically possible to do many custom things with the library's Facebook Wall, including replicating some complex functionality normally associated with websites, it's almost certainly not worth the time of most libraries to bother. Brand Glue, a company that manages pages for other companies, has studied the issue by mining Facebook API data; it found that 99.5 percent of all comments on status updates actually come from within people's news feeds, not directly on a company or organization's wall. Typically, the only time your library's fans will actually visit your library's wall directly is when they first "like" the page. This means the vast majority of customizations of Facebook Pages are largely useless.

Jay Baer, social media content strategist, says:

> Just because you CAN replicate much of your corporate website functionality on Facebook, doesn't mean you SHOULD. Your Facebook fan page is not a collectible automobile. You do not get

extra brand advocacy points for fuzzy dice, pin stripes, a chrome engine or a bitchin' stereo.[13]

Libraries are better off spending more time ensuring their content is seen by others in their news feeds and that, when it is seen, it's designed to engage the viewer. Aside from the initial clicking of the "Like" button, attempting to draw more attention to (and trying to get others to visit) the library's page is wasted effort.

BOTTOM LINE ▶ For most libraries, extensive customization of Facebook Pages or attempting to make the page act like your library's website is often a way to sap staff time with no likely ROI.

THINGS THAT WORK

All of the best practices discussed in chapter 4 will still apply to working with your library's Facebook account. But because of the much more interactive nature of Facebook than many other networks and the many additional capabilities offered, libraries also need to be aware of strategies that apply specifically to Facebook. This is especially true considering the constantly changing interface of the site and the continued research that's being done on what is effective use of it.

The following information may help your library think about what it can do to maximize its presence on Facebook:

- *Time it properly.* A 2011 study by Buddy Media found that Facebook engagement peaks at three different times of day: early morning (7 a.m. EST), after work (5 p.m. EST), and late evenings (around 11 p.m. EST).[14] If your library posts all of its updates only during the typical 9–5 (EST) workday, it will be missing what is essentially prime time hours on Facebook. The study found that brands that posted outside of regular business hours had an engagement rate averaging 20 percent higher than if they posted only during traditional day times.
- *Length matters.* The same study found the length of a post can determine potential responses just as much as the timing. Those with eighty characters or less received 27 percent more engagement than those that were longer. Conversely, URLs included in Facebook posts should actually be *longer.* Posts with a full-length URL, as opposed to

those that use a URL shortener, such as bit.ly or tinyurl, got three times the amount of engagement. The probable reason is that people like to know where a URL will take them before they click on it. Joe Ciarallo, Buddy Media's director of communications, says that a brand-specific URL shortener, such as one used by Mashable.com (on.mash), keeps posts short while still providing some context for the user.[15]

- *Involve your fans.* Periodically, be sure to ask your library's fans questions about themselves. Ask them to share their own favorite content with the library. This practice is simply good social media work—starting conversations and not talking entirely about oneself. Again, be careful about stale, boring questions often used by libraries, such as "What is your favorite book?" Remember, your library is often competing with dozens, if not hundreds, of other items streaming by on a user's wall. Be creative.

- *Use the right words when asking for engagement.* Data from the Buddy Media study makes it clear that asking outright for feedback is actually quite effective, especially if the correct word choice is used. The most effective word was found to be *post,* followed by *comment* and *tell us,* respectively. However, Ciarallo cautions against asking users to tell you anything that answers a why question: these kinds of requests may seem more invasive to the visitor and also require more thought than many people may want to give.[16]

- *Make friends with multimedia.* Ekaterina Walter is a social media strategist at Intel. Walter says: "Media like videos and photos always perform well on Facebook. Not only do they seem to be a favorite of the News Feed algorithm, but they just grab people's attention in a feed full of text updates. A lot of web users choose to *watch* more than they *read.*"[17] Such a statement illustrates the proverb: a picture (or video) is worth a thousand words. Pictures and videos are also the kind of value-added content that many expect from companies and organizations on Facebook—the kind of thing they don't get ordinarily from more text-based sites, such as Twitter or even blogs. Facebook also makes these kinds of things incredibly easy to share, making this kind of content potentially twice as powerful, since it can quickly be spread to a user's Facebook community.

- *Tag people.* Facebook offers an easy way to mark photos with users' names, and this process also results in the marked users getting a message that they've been "tagged." If your library is uploading patron photos, be sure to find out if they're on Facebook so you can tag them. This is a great way of interacting with individual patrons, who will in turn be likely to share that content out to their own friends.

- *Vary your content.* Don't be afraid to change up your content occasionally. If you are regularly posting photos from your library's events, don't be afraid to do something different. If your library just got a new self-check machine, take a photo and challenge people to see what's different in the library. Explain in the caption what the new machine does and how it makes service better. If you see something interesting in someone else's news feed, have the library share it on its own wall (and give credit to the originator, of course). Remember that your content cannot be all about the library strictly promoting programs: this tunnel-vision focus provides no value to the library's fans and violates all of the tenets of effective social media.

- *Quiz people.* Testing fans' knowledge with a relevant quiz or quiz-type questions can be fun and also encourage people to respond. Try a weekly feature where people have to guess the answer to something library related, and where the answer will pique their interest. "Our library's director has a unique hobby. Hint: she stomps her feet a lot." (Answer: Irish stepdancing.) Some guesses may just be silly, but if the library responds lightheartedly, this can do much to show that the library has a human voice in social media. People like organizations that have a sense of humor.

- *Thank one fan in a really big way—publicly.* The NBA is on the leading edge of thanking their fans via social media. Any company could give away coupons, tickets, or other swag, but the NBA has gone one step further. They thank select fans with personalized videos by some of their biggest athletic stars. Is an author or local celebrity coming to visit the library? Ask if they will record a very short video (no more than thirty seconds) thanking a special patron. The patron could be randomly picked, or the winner of a contest of some sort. Either way, be sure to post the video on Facebook—and be sure to stipulate that winners had to have "liked" the library on Facebook as well in order to win. The winner will almost certainly share that video out to his or her friends.

BOTTOM LINE ▶ Boring, stagnant content will get your library little or nothing that will help it meet its social media goals. Time your content appropriately and specifically request engagement from your Facebook fans.

THINGS THAT DON'T WORK

Some common practices on Facebook can actually be counterproductive. Be sure that your library is familiar with these things that generally don't bring any return on investment, or can even be damaging to your library's image on Facebook:

- *Don't automate.* There are several Facebook apps that allow you to automatically pull the tweets from your library's Twitter account or your library's blog and have them post to your Facebook Wall. This is problematic on several levels. Firstly, the algorithm that determines what goes into users' news feeds generally discriminates against automated content.[18] This means your automated posts will likely never have been seen by anyone. Secondly, while this method does save time for your library, it is not respectful of the time of your library's fans. Use customized posts for each. Ekaterina Walter of Intel says: "You will get far better engagement and show your fans you care. Some folks who use Facebook don't really like Twitter and get irritated when they see hashtags or other Twitter-specific content in their Facebook stream."[19]
- *Forget the video or photo contests.* Peter Yared is the vice president and general manager of Webtrend Apps, a platform used by top brands to engage their customers on Facebook, iPhone, and Android. Yared points out that uploading photos and videos is a substantial investment for users, and many organizations and companies simply do not have a following willing to bother. He recommends that, if you feel you must do this, to do it more informally, using Facebook's built-in photo capabilities. Have users upload content to the library's page, where the library can moderate it. Users can then share their items with their friends and ask them in turn to "like" them. This method means that more contest-related content will show up in others news feeds and takes advantage of the potentially viral channels that can be built on Facebook.
- *Avoid "like" blocking.* A like block is when a user has to "like" a Facebook Page in order to see certain content. Yared says that in his work, he sees an average of a 50 percent drop-off rate when like blocks are used, even when the content is worth it, such as a really good coupon. Putting a like block on basic content (your library's

"normal" stuff) will, in Yared's words, "almost guarantee a 100% drop-off rate."[20]

BOTTOM LINE ▶   Peter Yared sums it up: "A brand on Facebook should be like a casual friend or neighbor and not try to suck people into heavy levels of interaction. What do you do with a friend? Comment on their photos, like their status, vote on their outfit. These types of interactions take seconds, not minutes, and definitely not hours."[21]

MAKING THE MOST OF FACEBOOK EVENTS

Although the Events feature of Facebook has been around for some time, it seems that few libraries take advantage of it. Mari Smith, the coauthor of *Facebook Marketing: An Hour a Day,* calls the Events application "one of the most powerful tools of the platform and there is a fine art to using it effectively."[22] Smith also recommends that event promoters use the following strategies to make the most of this tool:

- *Go with the default settings.* When you create a Facebook Event, you have many options to limit how the event information is seen and interacted with. Allow guests to invite other people, leave comments, and provide photos and links of their own. The guests who do these things will create more visibility for your event, since all of these items will then show up in their own news feeds and those of their friends.
- *Create a catchy title and subtitle, and be sure to include a photo or image.* These three fields are the only ones that actually appear in "Requests" when people are invited.
- *Comment on your own Event Wall.* If someone RSVPs for your library's event and leaves a comment or other piece of content on the event's page, be sure to respond. Smith also suggests thanking people personally on their own walls for coming. All of these activities are also pushed out to people's news feeds.

Once an event is created, a button will be available that says "Update Fans of [YOUR PAGE NAME]." Be sure to use this so that the event is promoted directly to the people who "like" your library on Facebook. Include a short message and catchy title. This sends a direct message to the fans of your library, and shows up in their Facebook inboxes. They, in turn, can choose to share out the event information on their own walls.

After the event, be sure to upload lots of photos to your library's Facebook Page. Encourage the library's fans to tag themselves if they appear in any of them. This, in turn, will result in the photos also appearing on *their* walls and in their friends' news feeds. This is additional, free exposure for the library.

BOTTOM LINE ▸ Events can be a powerful Facebook tool to promote programs and provoke additional patron engagement. When creating events, spend time making sure that they sound and look appealing, and that there is follow-up afterward for even more opportunities for conversations.

WORKING WITH FACEBOOK INSIGHTS

One of the most powerful features of Facebook is Facebook Insights, a built-in analytics application that is only available to page administrators. (One caveat: Insights is only available for pages that have thirty or more fans.) Insights provides metrics that can demonstrate trends on your page, including those concerning the creation of content and how it is being consumed by fans. Insights is typically divided into metrics for users and for interactions, and activity in both areas can be seen in monthly or even daily increments. Data can be exported as a CSV (comma-separated values) file—a common format that can usually be easily imported into common spreadsheet programs like Microsoft Excel.

Facebook Insights also provides some basic information about how individual posts perform. When you are logged in as the page's administrator, you will see two statistics immediately below each post: impressions and feedback. The number of impressions is the number of times that piece of content has been viewed anywhere on Facebook. Impressions is not the same as the number of *people* who viewed the post; people may view the same post multiple times. Feedback, given as a percentage, is the amount of interaction around that content, based on the number of people who saw it (impressions). Feedback only measures "likes" and comments; it doesn't measure video plays or other forms of interaction.

The value of Insights quickly becomes apparent when evaluating which kinds of posts generate the most interaction. Knowing what types of content interest your fans the most allows your library to be the most efficient with what it posts to Facebook. It might seem likely that people respond better to a posted photo than to a text-based post, but until you see the numbers, it is only an unconfirmed guess. In particular, keep an eye on the long-term trends; what happens day-to-day may not reflect real fan preferences and may only show what was popular to the people who paid attention that day. Being aware of what your fans like most gives your library the ability to give its fans what they want and can also save your library considerable time and effort.

One metric in particular that libraries should pay attention to is daily active users. This is anyone who has commented, visited, or liked your content each day. This will give you a much clearer picture of your actual traffic on Facebook. Your library may have hundreds, or even thousands, of fans, but that number holds no meaning if none of them visits your page again or interacts with your library's content. A daily active user is anyone that has commented, visited, or liked your page each day. If this number is lower than you are comfortable with, that's probably a good indicator your library needs to change what it posts. It's also helpful to pay attention to when this number spikes. Are weekends better times to get feedback? This kind of information can help determine your library's Facebook strategy as it progresses.

Metrics for Facebook are mostly (and perhaps only) valuable over the long term. Each of Insight's sections can be used to monitor how your page is performing on a daily or monthly basis, but it's the overall trends that will matter most. As long as the numbers are progressing upward, your library can probably consider its presence there a success.

BOTTOM LINE ▸ Don't ignore the available Facebook Insights numbers. They are very valuable for fine-tuning your library's Facebook work and should be tracked over time to see real fan preferences.

PROMOTING YOUR PAGE OUTSIDE OF FACEBOOK

Building a page on Facebook is not at all like the film *Field of Dreams:* "If you build it, they will come." Simply creating the page is far from enough to get people to like your library on Facebook. It's going to require continual effort on your part to ensure a steady stream of new people are even made aware your library exists on the social network (and it's reasonable to assume some will, invariably, migrate away for one reason or another). Following are some ways that your library can bring in new followers:

- *Don't be afraid to promote to your library's current newsletter subscribers.* If your library e-mails a newsletter to its patrons, this is the perfect opportunity to make them aware they can find their local library on Facebook. In each issue, include a small blurb or even the Facebook logo and ask patrons to click the included link to get to your library's page. Ask them directly to "like" the library on Facebook. Even if your library doesn't send out digital newsletters, it can do essentially the same thing in print. Include the vanity URL you created with the blurb or icon so people have an easy link they can type in to find your library. Be sure to include this call to action in *each* issue of the newsletter. John Haydon, a social media and marketing expert who works with nonprofits, says: "Most times, people need to see a call to action multiple times before they like your Page. Design your email template with a link to your Facebook Page in the sidebar. This way it's included in every email."[23] Use this strategy for print as well as digital communications.
- *Promote it on the footer of your website and blog.* Many people look for additional information about an organization in the footer of websites and blogs. Be sure to include a prominent Facebook logo, linked directly to your library's page.
- *Use it for blog fodder.* If someone posts something interesting to your library's page, use it as the foundation for a blog post. Cross-link between the page and the blog post for optimized traffic between the two.
- *Get them when they're thinking about the library.* Does your library have an online form that allows people to sign up for library cards or online registration? Offer people the chance to "like" your library after they complete the forms and while you're thanking them for completing the form.
- *Consider putting the vanity URL and/or Facebook logo on business cards and other print materials.* Doing so carries the message to more places and more consistently. Remember, people may need exposure to a message over and over before they act on it. While you're thinking about this suggestion, also consider the idea of adding these to the e-mail signatures of library staff.
- *Promote your page at the circulation and reference desks.* Put a placard where people can see it—at points in your physical library where they interact the most. Elevators are also a good place to put a sign. You

may even want to expand on this; if they join right away via a library computer or mobile device, offer some kind of instant incentive.

- *Cross-promote on Twitter.* If your library has a Twitter account, you can use it to promote the Facebook Page. However, be cautious; don't just blare "Like us on Facebook!" That does not give any reason for people to buy in. Instead, try promoting individual posts that may be of interest to the Twitter audience.

- *Try a Facebook plug-in.* There are many widgets that can easily be embedded in your library's websites or blogs (see the full list at https://developers.facebook.com/docs/plugins/). The LikeBox allows people to "like" your library's page from outside Facebook (although they will still need to log in) and also shows how many other people "like" your page as well. They can also see the most recent posts. Additionally, there are plug-ins that allow visitors to make comments on your sites using their Facebook profile or easily send your library's web content to their friends.

SOME FINAL WORDS ABOUT FACEBOOK

When posting any kind of content to social media channels, it's critical to remind yourself the primary reason for doing so is not to broadcast a message, but to create interactions. This is especially important on Facebook. A salient fact to remember in this regard is this one: The most-cited reason for unfriending people (and, by extension, "unliking" pages) is because people perceive too many posts to be useless.[24] Whatever your library posts, it has to possess some obvious value to the recipients. Talk *to* and *with* your audience, but not *at* them.

People become fans of a Facebook Page for varying reasons: because someone asked them, because one of their friends is, or perhaps just because it's easy to do. However, it's only with the people who *genuinely* like or are interested in your library that you are likely to have a high number of interactions.[25] Your library may grow to have a large number of fans, but many of those will never contribute to or initiate any dialogue. This is why numbers of fans or followers in social media are largely meaningless—only those who actively participate are generally meaningful. Facebook allows for many different ways to create exchanges with your library's patrons. Focus on finding the ones that work for your library and get the best results.

NOTES

1. Darren Waddell, "Social Marketing Continues Meteoric Rise among Local Businesses," *MerchantCircle Press Releases,* February 15, 2011, www.merchantcircle.com/corporate/press/2011-01-15-social-marketing-continues-meteoric-rise-among-local-businesses.html.

2. *Facebook Factsheet,* Facebook, www.facebook.com/press/info.php?factsheet (accessed July 21, 2011).

3. Xavier Lur, "If Facebook Were a Country, It Would Be the 3rd Most Populated," March 19, 2010, www.techxav.com/2010/03/19/if-facebook-were-a-country.

4. *Facebook Statistics,* Facebook, www.facebook.com/press/info.php?statistics (accessed July 21, 2011).

5. Ibid.

6. Ibid.

7. Cory Doctorow, "How to say stupid things about social media," *The Guardian,* January 5, 2010, www.guardian.co.uk/technology/2010/jan/05/social-media-cory-doctorow.

8. *Facebook Help Center,* Facebook, www.facebook.com/help/?faq=12320 (accessed July 21, 2011).

9. Curt Hopkins, "Facebook's Community Pages Unleashed Upon World," April 19, 2010, www.readwriteweb.com/archives/facebooks_community_pages_unleashed_upon_world.php.

10. John Paul Titlow, "How to Convert a Facebook Profile to a Page," *ReadWriteWeb,* March 10, 2011, www.readwriteweb.com/biz/2011/03/how-to-convert-a-facebook-profile-to-a-page.php.

11. Lauren Drell, "Facebook Timeline: 9 Best Practices for Brands," *Mashable Business,* May 17, 2012, http://mashable.com/2012/05/17/facebook-timeline-brand-tips.

12. Sarah Kessler, "Facebook Timeline Changed the Way We See Brand Pages; Here's How," *Mashable Business,* April 30, 2012, http://mashable.com/2012/04/30/facebook-timeline-eyetrack-study.

13. Jay Baer, "Digital Sharecropping—Why Most Facebook Customization is Wasted Effort," *Convince & Convert,* October 27, 2010, www.convinceandconvert.com/social-media-marketing/digital-sharecropping-why-most-facebook-customization-is-wasted-effort.

14. Michael Lazerow, "Introducing Our Latest Research: 'Strategies for Effective Facebook Wall Posts: A Statistical Review,'" *Buddy Media,* April 6, 2011, www.buddymedia.com/newsroom/2011/04/introducing-our-latest-research-"strategies-for-effective-facebook-wall-posts-a-statistical-review"/.

15. Lauren Drell, "HOW TO: Improve Engagement on Your Brand's Facebook Page [STATS]," *Mashable Social Media,* April 6, 2011, http://mashable.com/2011/04/06/facebook-engagement-data.

16. Ibid.

17. Ekaterina Walter, "10 Tips for Posting on Your Brand's Facebook Page," *Mashable Social Media,* March 22, 2011, http://mashable.com/2011/03/22/tips-brand-facebook-page.

18.   Ibid.

19.   Ibid.

20.   Peter Yared, "Why Most Facebook Marketing Doesn't Work," *ReadWriteWeb*, February 17, 2011, www.readwriteweb.com/archives/why_most_facebook_marketing_doesnt_work.php.

21.   Ibid.

22.   Mari Smith, "10 Tips for Creating Buzz with Facebook Events," *Social Media Examiner*, October 29, 2009, www.socialmediaexaminer.com/10-tips-for-creating-buzz-with-facebook-events.

23.   John Haydon, "11 ways to promote your Facebook Page outside Facebook," June 11, 2010, www.johnhaydon.com/2010/06/11-ways-promote-facebook-page-facebook.

24.   Bob Brown, "Top reason for Facebook unfriending: Too many useless posts," *Network World*, October 5, 2010, www.networkworld.com/news/2010/100510-facebook-unfriending-colorado.html.

25.   Aliza Sherman, "5 Things That Don't Work on Facebook Pages (and 5 That Do)," *GigaOm Web Worker Daily*, March 31, 2010, http://gigaom.com/collaboration/5-things-that-dont-work-on-facebook-pages-and-5-that-do.

TEENS AND SOCIAL MEDIA

Testing Assumptions

The problem with Facebook? Moms. "My mom uses it to plan dinner" was the sound bite complaint. Or "My great aunt from Canada friended me the other day." One [attendee] remarked that he would pay his mom money to get OFF Facebook.

—COMMENTS FROM THE "WHAT DO TEENS WANT?"
PANEL AT THE 2009 WEB 2.0 SUMMIT[1]

When speaking with librarians, it's not uncommon to find that many primarily associate social media specifically with younger patrons, especially teens and tweens. There is a clear understanding that kids are heavy users of social media, and there's certainly some validity to this. Seventy-three percent of youth ages 12–17 use social media.[2] More than fourteen million of Facebook's U.S. user base is between the ages of 13 and 17.[3] Widespread assumptions that correlate teens with social media are, generally speaking, correct. Many librarians also believe that social media is, therefore, the ideal way to reach out to this demographic. However, that premise, along with several others relating to teens and social media use, may be flawed. What follows is an examination of some of these beliefs, as well as some suggestions for using social media effectively with this age group.

WHAT ARE THEY ACTUALLY USING?

Pinning down the social media sites on which teens and tweens are most active can be somewhat tricky. It wasn't so long ago that MySpace was the online destination of choice; now many teens actively avoid it. Where are they now? Without a doubt (at least as of this writing), the answer is clear: Facebook. Seventy-eight percent of teens have a Facebook profile and 69 percent of those are active users. YouTube usage comes in second, at 64 percent of teens having a profile. MySpace now ranks third at only 41 percent.[4] Linda Bissell, age 17, says that she much prefers Facebook to MySpace. Not only is that where her friends are now, but she found MySpace to be too disorganized. The ability to change backgrounds and designs of a MySpace page was appealing, but overall, users wasted too much time and it made the site harder to use.[5]

The extent of Facebook's popularity among the teen population is perhaps most easily seen in the number of *illegal* accounts created by younger kids. According to the social network, it bans 20,000 users a day for being below the age requirement (13 years old).[6] *Consumer Reports* estimated some 7.5 million Facebook users are underage.[7] Kids want to be where other kids are, or where they perceive the popular crowd to be, and the large number of underage accounts demonstrates this proclivity. The survey from *Consumer Reports* also found that the majority of parents of kids 10 and under were generally not concerned by their children's use of Facebook.[8] It seems likely parents also recognize the increasing of ubiquity of Facebook in young people's lives and support their children's use of it.

But what about Twitter? For those libraries who have adopted Twitter primarily for communication with teens, they are no doubt going to be disappointed. According to the Pew Internet & American Life Project, teens ages 12–17 do not use Twitter in large numbers. Only 8 percent of teens in this group even use it.[9] "This puts Twitter far down the list of popular online activities for teens and stands in stark contrast to their record of being early adopters of nearly every online activity."[10] The vast majority of Twitter users are in adult demographics, age 18 and older.

The ways in which Twitter is most often used by adults are often not applicable to teens. Most adult users of Twitter tweet either for self-promotion or to follow their interests and specific types of news. Teens use online social platforms as a way to keep up with their circle of friends. Twitter is a public broadcast of information, to people who are not necessarily friends but rather a broad audience. Michael Moore-Jones, a 16-year-old guest writer for ReadWriteWeb, sums it up: "Twitter is a platform built for inclusive broadcast (to everyone), and to teenagers it offers no obvious value."[11] He goes on to say: "Teenagers don't usually care about being updated in real time on current events, and those events that are big enough, or relevant to them, will be shared by their real friends. It's the simple fact that Twitter isn't solving a problem that teenagers have, so there is no need for it."[12]

Some teens, however, do use Twitter, but for very personalized uses. Derek Stillman, a high school senior from Willoughby, Ohio, uses Twitter as a way to do effective group messaging. Derek became very frustrated when he needed to text a message to multiple friends simultaneously. He convinced his friends to get Twitter accounts and subscribe to his tweets. Now, his entire group can send group messages using Twitter. Derek chose Twitter primarily because it was a good option for his friends, all of whom own cell phones and use them primarily to text. Derek's friends do not use Twitter to get news at all; rather, this use of the microblogging site is a planned workaround to the obstacles of communicating easily with a group via texting. Annie Cahill, 17, has an additional use of Twitter: her boss from her after-school job uses it to send group messages to employees. This is another form of group messaging and not a typical use for Twitter. If your library's teen librarian (or department) is currently using Twitter, it is likely an effort that's not going to see a justifiable return on investment.

Blogging is another area where teen participation is extremely limited—and still declining. With the advent of social media and the ability to communicate feelings and updates directly to one's friends, social media has replaced much of the need for teenagers to blog. There has been a dramatic decrease in blogging among teenagers: 28 percent of teens reported to Pew that they blogged in 2006. That number has since dropped to only 14 percent in 2010.[13] Teens can keep their friends updated about their lives via Facebook, with far less effort than blogging and with more regularity.

BOTTOM LINE Teens are on Facebook. If your library currently attempts to lure teens via Twitter, it is probably a wasted effort, especially considering the limited number of teens who even use it, and even fewer who use it in the typical manner. Blogging is also no longer popular with teens, who are not heavy content creators.

HOW DO TEENS FEEL ABOUT FACEBOOK?

Facebook is certainly a major facet of many teenagers' lives. It's a major sacrifice to go without logging in for many of them. In 2010, many teens gave Facebook up for Lent.[14] When high school senior Derek Stillman was asked if he would ever give up Facebook, his reply was, "Only if everyone else does!"

A study by the Henry J. Kaiser Family Foundation found that 15- to 18-year-olds who do social networking spend an average of forty-eight minutes a day on social media sites.[15] It's safe to assume that a large part of that time was being spent on Facebook.

As vital as Facebook can be to the lives of so many teens, their feelings about it can be somewhat ambivalent. Courtney Misich, age 18, points out that "life before social media was much easier—you knew who your true friends were."[16] Her friend, Jaclyn Gleske, feels similarly: "Relationships are less personal."[17] It's not uncommon to find, especially among older teens who remember life before social media, that they recall those Facebook-free days as being simpler and as having had more free time. "A lot of drama starts on Facebook," says Karen Bissell, 15. Relationships have also become more complex as a result of the site. Emily Hooley, 16, points out that fights do happen on Facebook, and the aftermath can be difficult:

> It's weird. If I have a massive fight on Facebook, it's always, like, the next day, did it actually matter? Was it important? I always go up to the person afterwards and talk to them face-to-face, to see their emotions and their expressions. Otherwise you never know. It's complicated.[18]

Relationships with peers are not the only complexity that teens have to deal with when using Facebook. Parents, too, constitute obstacles that may have to be negotiated. Linda Bissell says, "My dad stalks us," referring to the Facebook accounts of both her and her sister, Karen. Some teens, like David Gardner, 17, block their parents altogether by simply ignoring friend requests. Sometimes, parental involvement can even drive teens away from Facebook. A 2010 poll by online gaming site Roiworld found that 16 percent of respondents either decreased Facebook use or left it entirely because of their parents joining the site.[19] Yet parents are becoming more involved with children's social media use. A survey of 2,000 parents and teens by TRUST3 and Lightspeed Research found that 72 percent of parents check on the teens social media accounts at least once per month.[20] Despite this, most parents (84 percent) surveyed actually felt pretty confident in how their teens use social networking.

Some teens have close relationships with their parents and don't mind having them as Facebook friends; some even use the site as a way to keep their extended family informed of their day-to-day activities. Derek Stillman, 18, relies heavily on Facebook for exactly this. For him, it's an easy way to keep everyone in the loop about his life. Sometimes, this backfires on him. Derek tells of his grandmother, who is on Facebook and who attempts to friend his friends and makes odd comments on their walls. This situation is often hard to contend with, and he hasn't found a solution for it yet. Nonetheless, Derek is undeterred in his use of Facebook as a direct way to communicate regularly with so many people.

Maintaining one's friends list can also be a chore. Deciding how to add friends is a personal decision for each teen. If someone sends a friend request to Linda, she'll add them only if she knows them or they have mutual friends. David says that he will often accept friend requests from "weirdos," mostly because he is curious and wants to see their status updates. Surprisingly, teens also have to make decisions about unfriending. "You have to weed," says Annie Cahill, 17. Annie's specific policy about unfriending is if the person's birthday comes up in her Facebook calendar and she doesn't know the person, she unfriends them. (One of Annie's friends commented, "That's harsh! You unfriend them on their *birthday?*") Many times, unfriending may go unnoticed because the unfriended person may have too many friends already to notice when the count drops by one. Even if the person notices, it may be nearly impossible to figure out who the unfriender actually was.

BOTTOM LINE ▶ Facebook is essential for most teenagers, but represents varying relationship challenges for many of them.

TEENS AND PRIVACY

Conventional wisdom holds that young people are less concerned about their online privacy than older generations. Newer research, however, is beginning to show us that the exact opposite is true. In 2010, the Pew Internet & American Life Project found that people in their twenties are much more likely to actively protect their online information than their older counterparts.[21] The University of California, Berkeley, found that more than half of the young adults surveyed feel more concerned about online privacy than they did five years ago.[22] Even though that research was directed at a slightly older demographic than teens, it does show an ongoing trend: these younger users, who are also heavy participants in social media, are thinking more about privacy and bucking the accepted hypothesis that younger generations don't care about it. Laura M. Holson reports in the *New York Times* that Helen Nissenbaum, a professor of culture, media, and communication at New York University and author of the book *Privacy in Context,* says that "teenagers were naturally protective of their privacy as they navigate the path to adulthood, and the frequency with which companies change privacy rules has taught them to be wary."[23]

These younger users are keeping up-to-date with changing privacy settings and concerns through, of course, social media. Teens rely on their network of peers to let them know about news that may affect them. If a friend of a teen warns them about upcoming changes to the Facebook privacy settings, they are likely going to pay attention.

Teens have also come up with some innovative ways to protect their Facebook privacy in the digital age, even going beyond the available settings to do so. Here are some of the more common permutations:

- *Super-logoff.* Generally, when you log off of Facebook, you leave and your profile is still available. When you use the super-logoff method, you deactivate your account entirely, until you log in again. The profile is no longer available, and your Facebook presence is literally erased from Facebook—temporarily. No one can post anything to the profile's wall, send messages, or tag pictures since it's no longer "out there." No one can even see the content. Super-logoff enables you to have a sense of complete control when you aren't actually on Facebook. Some teens use this method for greater peace of mind—no one can do anything while they're not there. Others use it more purposefully, deactivating their account during final exams, for example. If their account is deactivated, they don't get constant messages from Facebook about their friends' activities. It's a way for them to control potential distractions when they should be studying. They can reactivate the account after their exams simply by logging in.
- *Whitewalling.* This method is much more time-consuming than that of the super-logoff. With whitewalling, you erase each post or comment after you are "done" sharing it. This prevents the particular content from being available via Facebook in the future. It can also be a way for some teens to reduce "undesirable" content on their profiles. Derek uses a form of whitewalling when he untags photos of him that others have taken in which he feels he doesn't look very good, and these pictures don't show up on his profile.
- *Secret messages.* With so many teens having to friend their parents on Facebook, many have struggled to find ways to communicate

personal things to their friends without their parents understanding what they're saying. For many, this method has been a form of steganography—hiding one message inside of another message. Researcher danah boyd has called this "social steganography." Typically, these kinds of status updates have two meanings: a simple, obvious meaning and the deeper, truer one. The most common approach is to use song lyrics. The use of particular lyrics may clue friends in on what a teen is feeling at the moment, or may indicate something else entirely. The lyrics, as isolated text, may not mean what the entire song actually means. Researcher boyd interviewed a girl who was dealing with a breakup on a class trip. She wanted her friends to know, but not her mother, who would have reacted badly. The girl posted the chorus to a humorous Monty Python song, sung by some men who have been crucified: "Always look on the bright side of life!" Her friends were fans of the film and realized that she was saying that she was going through something negative. Her mother, on the other hand, not knowing the movie, posted a response saying that she was glad her daughter was happy.[24] Many teens are familiar with pop culture and can use this tactic successfully to hide their true intent when they post.

Song lyrics do not always contain a hidden message, but can simply be an expression of a teen's feelings at the time. Teens can also use them to more easily express thoughts if they've been in a fight with one of their friends, giving them an easy way to find words that can be used in a public forum. They can also use lyrics simply as a way to get "likes" on their posts. "It can get obnoxious if someone uses them too often, though," says Annie.

BOTTOM LINE Teens, for the most part, are at least beginning to be seriously concerned about their privacy and have found some interesting ways to hide their content from the eyes of others. If your library communicates with teens on Facebook, be aware of these practices so you don't become unduly upset when teens use these tactics.

WHAT ABOUT THE LIBRARY?

The majority of teens use the Internet and are in constant contact with their friends via social media. "Whether they're connected via their phones,

"Any teens down there?"

gaming consoles, laptops or the computer lab at school, they're online pretty much all of the time. Social networking—on Facebook and elsewhere—is a huge part of what they're doing," says Read-WriteWeb writer John Paul Titlow.[25] Many libraries believe that social media is one of the best ways to engage with their teen patrons. Unfortunately, the research does not support this belief. Forrester Research, in March 2011, found this age group is even more likely than the 18–24 demographic to routinely post status updates to social networks. Yet Forrester also found that only 6 percent of U.S. consumers ages 12–17 are interested in engaging with brands on Facebook, even though they are active users of the site in general.[26]

The problem is often this: teens want to *initiate* discussions around products and brands; they don't want the brand or organization to do so. Forrester also learned that teen expectations of brands are not reciprocal. Only 16 percent want companies to interact with them using social tools, yet 28 percent expect companies to listen to what they're saying on social networks.[27] What's more problematic for libraries looking to use social media with teens is that almost half of teens don't even think that brands should have a presence in social media at all.[28] Most of them expect to use social networks to communicate with their real-life friends, not with companies or organizations.

This data undoubtedly constitutes a huge disappointment for many librarians. Traditional thought has held that social media is the ideal communication channel for libraries, since teens are already there in large numbers. This is not the case. What should libraries do? Following are a few suggestions:

- *Seriously reconsider having a social media account that is only geared toward teens.* If your library currently has, for example, a Facebook account just for its teen department, it's extremely unlikely that it will be worth the time to maintain it.

- *Don't pull your library entirely off of the social network.* Remember, some teens will still expect your library to have a channel open where it can listen. Think of it as having an open-door policy—nobody might take advantage of it, but someone may.
- *Move to a reactive stance.* Be more prepared to respond than to initiate conversations. This is completely contrary to everything you've learned thus far about social media, yet it may serve you to be flexible when it comes to dealing with teenagers. Be sure to respond to any questions or comments as quickly as possible.
- *Try a (very) different approach.* This method requires a library to get one or more staff members much more personally involved with the effort to recruit teens via social media (see "Doing It Differently," following).

Doing It Differently

Teen librarian Justin Hoenke is all too aware that teens are hard to engage online. His library, Portland Public Library (Maine), has a Facebook Page just for teens. Hoenke estimates that only 1 or maybe 2 percent of the kids who "like" the page actually interact with any content posted on it. Yet more than 300 teens have clicked the "Like" button, and Hoenke says that he's found Facebook to be a successful way to continue to engage with his young adult patrons. How can this be?

It would seem that Hoenke has inherently understood that teens don't really want to interact with faceless organizations. He takes a very different approach: he uses his personal Facebook profile to connect to kids. He only friends teens that he knows in person from the library. By using his personal account, Hoenke says that it has made a noticeable impact for him and the library.

> The discussion of personal and professional profiles always comes up. I didn't want to have two profiles (done it before, hated it) so I had to make a decision: add teens to my own accounts or hide myself far, far away. I went with what some may consider to be the unpopular route. I added them to my own accounts. I feel like it has made a world of difference.
>
> I am happy to share the real Justin with the teens that I serve. I have nothing bad to hide and all good to share. Letting them in on

my "personal" life has actually allowed me to establish a deeper connection with them. For example, when one teen found that him and I shared an interest in The Mars Volta, he came running in the library one day in disbelief. He was excited that I was into the same music as him. He now comes in a few times each week and we spend a good fifteen minutes or so talking about music.

This is just one of countless examples of how opening up my personal social networking accounts to teens has made it easier for me to connect with them and provide them with quality service. In the end, it makes you more of a real person to them. They become your friend and they trust you. The upside to this? They're using the library . . . and they love it.[29]

Hoenke often tells kids to "find him on Facebook" if they want to send him a message. Once a teen becomes his Facebook friend, Hoenke will ask the teen to also click the "Like" button on the library's page.

BOTTOM LINE ▶ Don't knock yourself out trying to get teenagers to "like" your library on Facebook or follow you anywhere online. The majority are simply not interested and may even resent your presence there at all. Instead, make productive use of your library's time by concentrating on responding when they initiate an interaction.

NOTES

1. Alexa Tsotsis, "What Do Teens Want? Their Moms Off Facebook," *SF Weekly*, October 22, 2009, http://blogs.sfweekly.com/shookdown/2009/10/what_do_teens_want.php.

2. Kristin Purcell and Amanda Lenhart, "Trends in Teen Communication: Opportunities and Challenges for Public Health Campaigns," *Pew Internet*, September 29, 2010, http://pewinternet.com/Presentations/2010/Sep/ONDCP.aspx.

3. Ken Burbary, "Facebook Demographics Revisited—2011 Statistics," *Web Business by Ken Burbary*, March 7, 2011, www.kenburbary.com/2011/03/facebook-demographics-revisited-2011-statistics-2.

4. Jennifer Van Grove, "Teens Experiencing Facebook Fatigue [STUDY]," *Mashable Social Media*, June 30, 2010, http://mashable.com/2010/06/30/teens-social-networks-study.

5. Linda Bissell, personal interview, May 19, 2011.

6. "Facebook Bans 20,000 Kids a Day," *iSpyce*, March 23, 2011, http://ispyce.com/2011/03/facebook-bans-20000-kids-day.html.

7. Nicholas Kolakowski, "Facebook Filled with Underage, Unsupervised Users: Consumer Reports," *eWeek.com*, May 10, 2011, www.eweek.com/c/a/Web-Services -Web-20-and-SOA/Facebook-Filled-With-Underage-Supervised-Users-Consumer -Reports-416060.

8. Ibid.

9. Amanda Lenhart et al., "Social Media and Young Adults," *Pew Internet*, February 3, 2010, www.pewinternet.org/Reports/2010/Social-Media-and-Young-Adults.aspx.

10. Ibid.

11. Michael Moore-Jones, "Why Teens Don't and Won't Tweet," *ReadWriteWeb*, December 8, 2010, www.readwriteweb.com/archives/why_teens_dont_and_wont_ tweet.php.

12. Ibid.

13. Amanda Lenhart et al., "Social Media and Young Adults."

14. Meredith Heagney, "Teenagers unfriend Facebook for Lent." *The Columbus Dispatch*, February 19, 2010, Home ed., 01A.

15. Ibid.

16. Courtney Misich, personal interview, May 19, 2011.

17. Jaclyn Gleske, personal interview, May 19, 2011.

18. Jon Henley, "Teenagers and technology: 'I'd rather give up my kidney than my phone,'" *The Guardian*, July 16, 2010, www.guardian.co.uk/lifeandstyle/2010/jul/16/ teenagers-mobiles-facebook-social-networking?CMP=twt_iph.

19. Jennifer Van Grove, "Teens Experiencing Facebook Fatigue [STUDY]."

20. Adam Ostrow, "Hey, Teens: Your Parents Are Probably Checking Your Facebook [STUDY]," *Mashable Social Media*, October 20, 2010, http://mashable.com/2010/10/20/ parents-teens-facebook-monitoring.

21. Laura M. Holson, "Tell-All Generation Learns to Keep Things Offline," *New York Times*, May 8, 2010, www.nytimes.com/2010/05/09/fashion/09privacy.html.

22. Ibid.

23. Ibid.

24. Clive Thompson, "Clive Thompson on Secret Messages in the Digital Age," *Wired*, January 2011, www.wired.com/magazine/2011/01/st_thompson_secretmessages/.

25. John Paul Titlow, "Despite Living Online, Teenagers Don't Want to 'Like' Your Company on Facebook," *ReadWriteWeb*, March 8, 2011, www.readwriteweb.com/ biz/2011/03/despite-living-online-teenagers-dont-like-companies-on-facebook.php.

26. Ibid.

27. Ibid.

28. Mike Shields, "Young Users Hating on Brands," *Adweek*, March 9, 2011, www .adweek.com/news/advertising-branding/young-users-hating-brands-126346.

29. Justin Hoenke, "Using Social Media to Connect with Teens," *Tame the Web*, March 17, 2010, http://tametheweb.com/2010/03/17/using-social-media-to-connect-with-teens.

8

ONLINE REPUTATION MANAGEMENT

The moral of the story is that a single person can damage your brand, whether they work for your company or not. It doesn't matter if that brand is a company, product, or person, the results are real and it forces us all to have a reputation management strategy.

—DAN SCHAWBEL, AUTHOR OF *ME 2.0: 4 STEPS TO BUILDING YOUR FUTURE*

KEEPING AN EYE OUT

One of the best examples of what can go awry with a company's reputation is that of the #AmazonFAIL fiasco, as previously mentioned in chapter 4. In 2009, Amazon.com seemingly made a decision that caused a considerable and swift reaction around the Web. The sales rankings of hundreds of gay and lesbian themed books disappeared, with no forewarning. When writer Mark Probst contacted Amazon about the issue, he was informed by a representative that the company would no longer be including rankings for "adult" material.[1] People were angry over Amazon's apparent decision to group gay-themed books with pornography. Many people claimed it was a move toward censorship by Amazon.

However, this example shows more than just what happens when a company reacts slowly. The backlash by online communities was not only fast, it was extremely negative. This situation showed very clearly how much damage can be inflicted to a company's reputation, in a very short amount of time, with social media. Probst posted the story and Amazon's response on April 12, 2009. Within 24 hours, the following occurred:

- More than 5,000 related blog posts appeared across the Web. It was also the main story on the popular blog Techmeme.
- A Facebook group was launched, with more than 1,200 members joining immediately.
- Online petitions, asking for a reversal of Amazon's policy, appeared. One got more than 9,000 signatures in just a few hours.
- On Twitter, users began using #AmazonFAIL as a hashtag. It became the top trending term on Twitter that day.
- A premade template was created to allow people to more easily complain to Amazon.com.
- People began hacking gay-themed books on Amazon, by tagging them with #AmazonFAIL. Within hours, more than 800 books were tagged.
- Logos and merchandise appeared, all created by protesters.

Amazon later responded to this public relations crisis, saying that the issue was a technical error rather than a decision. This prompted a new hashtag around the Web, #glitchmyass, as well as a significant loss of trust and goodwill. Jackie Huba, of the *Church of the Customer Blog*, writes: "The anger of injustice spreads quickly and can take on a life of its own. For a company that helped pioneer using customer comments to sell books in a flattened, democratized context, this sure seemed like a fail moment for Amazon."[2]

The #AmazonFAIL crisis provides a valuable lesson for any business or organization. The situation spread globally, in mere hours. Tools such as Twitter have not only made this possible, they also have made it the norm. A good deal of news now breaks on Twitter before it makes it to a traditional media news source. Once news appears on Twitter, it's just a matter of time before people spread it to a wider audience. This reinforces the need to respond to criticism immediately. Before the advent of this medium, organizations often had the luxury of hours or days before needing to respond to a public relations crisis. Now, situations can escalate to global proportions within mere minutes.

Libraries need to be acutely aware of how fast negative feedback can spread and be prepared to deal with this new reality. The first step is for a library to understand at least some of the fundamental concepts of online reputation management (ORM). ORM is not just about monitoring your library's reputation online, it also involves knowing how to evaluate and react to any commentary on the Web about your library.

BOTTOM LINE ▶ Online reputation management (ORM) is just as critical for libraries as regular public relations. The time-sensitive nature of social media can quickly create PR disasters; monitoring online is the only way to get a heads-up as things happen.

FROM THE BEGINNING: THE RISK OF BRANDJACKING

Many libraries may have been reluctant to participate at all in social media, and unfortunately, this can come back to hurt them in significant ways. By not even creating accounts on major social media sites, these libraries open themselves up to brandjacking. There are various forms of brandjacking, but essentially it occurs when a person or organization loses control of its online presence.

When a library fails to create social media accounts, it's usually very simple for someone else to simply claim the library's name on that social media service. Very few social media sites have a process by which they verify the identity of the owner of an account. If your library does not create an account on YouTube, it could be a matter of moments before someone else claims that namespace and gives the account your library's name. What that person *does* with the account is almost secondary; the fact that the library's name is being used by an unrelated, unauthorized person is problematic enough. Even if the account sits unused, it's still a major issue that the library has no control over it. The account could be used for inappropriate content at any time, and forcing the removal of the account can range from difficult to impossible.

Even if your library makes the decision not to take part in social media, it's critical that it still claim its name on all of the major services. Even if your library never intends to start producing videos, claim the name on YouTube, Vimeo, and any other important video service. If your library decides it will use Facebook but not Twitter, be sure to still get the Twitter account. It's an all-too-simple matter for a disgruntled patron to imitate the library in social media; by claiming the library's online presence in social media channels, this becomes much harder to do.

Begin by using an online tool to determine if your library's name or vanity URL is available in various social network spaces; these exist so that you do not have to check with each service individually, which would be quite time consuming. Some free ones to try are as follows:

- Namechk.com (http://namechk.com): A very basic tool, checks approximately seventy-two of the more popular social networks for your name.
- Knowem.com (http://knowem.com): Searches more than 300 social media sites and also prioritizes by those that are currently the most popular. If you're willing to pay, this site will also automatically reserve your name on varying numbers of social networks.
- NameChecklist (www.namechecklist.com): Sorts results into social media, top-level domains (e.g., .com, .net, .org, etc.), and search engines and media (figure 8.1).

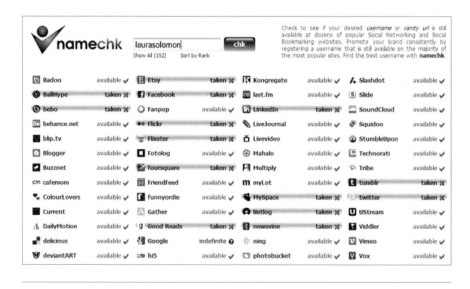

FIGURE 8.1 **Namechk.com results**

Brandjacking does not always involve using the library's name, however. Another form of brandjacking relates to losing control of an organization's message. This is a situation in which social media can turn truly ugly, and the #AmazonFAIL fiasco is a clear demonstration of it. It didn't involve any sort of technological theft, but instead relied on coordinated word-of-mouth vilification.

No library director wants to come in one morning and learn about the existence of a hashtag called "#mylibrarysucks." Like most things, prevention is better than dealing with a problem after it has occurred.

Aside from claiming social media namespaces, the most important thing your library can do to prevent a public relations disaster is to monitor what is being said about it online. Your library can't respond effectively to any criticism unless it first knows it exists. Monitoring your library's online reputation is crucial, and is often the first step toward managing your library's online reputation.

BOTTOM LINE While libraries no longer control their message in social media, it is crucial that they do not allow anyone else to control it. Make sure that your library claims profiles on all major social media sites, even if it does not intend to use them. Your library's name is valuable—claim it.

GETTING STARTED WITH MONITORING: WHAT'S THE AGENDA?

Before you begin any investigation of monitoring tools and practices, be sure that your library is very clear on the reasons *why* it is monitoring. Knowing the goals for monitoring social media is just as important as knowing why your library wants to participate in social media. Otherwise, how will your library know what it's really looking for?

Typically, reasons for monitoring may include:

- Hearing any bad or good commentary about the library
- Keeping current with trends that are being discussed (e.g., current events)
- Catching any service queries and being available at the point of need
- Seeing any discussions about the library and being able to quickly jump in, to bring more credibility to the library
- More than one of the above

If your library is monitoring social media for more than one of the listed reasons, it helps to know which ones are the most important. Understanding which has the most priority can assist with choosing which tools you'll use to monitor. Not all tools are ideal for each of these needs. Additionally, clearly recognizing what your library is looking for in the social media sphere can help focus its efforts so time and resources aren't wasted.

Keep in mind that all social media monitoring is done with an eye on responding rapidly to any question, crisis, or communication. To know about a mention or comment is only the beginning; engaging with the person who made it, quickly, is the library's primary goal.

BOTTOM LINE ▸ Your library needs to know not only why it's involved in social media, but also why it is monitoring it. Knowing what the end goal of the monitoring is will help your library figure out what tools it might need.

KEYWORDS: WHAT ARE YOU LOOKING FOR?

Once your library has decided on the reason *why* it is monitoring, the next step is to figure out *what* to monitor. Monitoring tools are typically based on the idea of watching for specific keywords. At the very least, your library should be listening for the following:

- Its name and any/all variants of its name
- Names of key administrators
- Your library's tagline
- Any keywords related to special promotions at your library

Some additional keyword categories your library may wish to track are the following:

- If your library is looking to gain a broader sense of how its public views related, third-party services, it may wish to also monitor mentions of a library's vendors (e.g., Overdrive, Tumblebooks).
- It may be helpful to track what other libraries are doing in social media. To get an idea of how often your library is mentioned, compared to others, try tracking keywords related to a similarly sized or nearby library.

BOTTOM LINE ▸ Most social media monitoring is about keeping a watch on specified keywords. Make sure your library has at least the basic ones covered.

CHOOSING MONITORING TOOLS

There are many monitoring tools for social media available, both of the free and fee-based varieties. If your library is working with a limited budget, it may be simple to look at those tools that have no cost involved. However, there are two important criteria that will apply to choosing any social monitoring tool or service.

First, consider what tools your library primarily uses. Some tools focus primarily on certain services, such as Facebook or Twitter. If your library is only participating in one or two social media sites, this may also help you to narrow your monitoring tool choices. That doesn't necessarily mean that you don't want to listen across other channels (e.g., only listening to Twitter if you don't participate with YouTube). The point of monitoring is to know what's being said about you online, after all. But if your library is mostly involved with, say, Twitter, having a tool that can center on that service may be helpful.

Second, remember what the metric goals are for your library. The tool your library picks needs to closely match its overall strategy. If your library wants to measure the number of Twitter mentions, make sure whichever service you choose has that capability. If your library has several measurements it wants to examine, it may find that it needs more than one service in order to track them.

Monitoring tools can also have different kinds of features that your library may find it prefers. Is there a need for a great deal of historical data? Do you want data in chart format? Does your library want clear indicators of "buzz" volume or the amount of influence any given commenter has? Monitoring services can vary widely not only in what kinds of data they monitor, but also in how they present their data and the context in which it might be presented.

Does your library desire some kind of sentiment analysis (knowing if comments are generally positive or negative)? This type of analysis is not always reliable; after all, it may not yet be reasonable to expect automated tools to figure out the actual meanings of human communication. While some tools do offer this kind of data, it would be wise to approach it with a great deal of caution.

Just as social media is a relatively new medium, new also are the tools developed to monitor it. Maria Ogneva, who is the director of social media at Attensity, writes:

Although there is no shortage of social media monitoring tools, each one is a bit different in its approach, methodology, metrics, depth of analysis, channels measured, reports and UI [user interface]. The existence of this many tools and the fragmentation of the tools market is evidence of the fact that the space is not quite mature, and doesn't yet have a set of agreed-upon metrics and best practices.[3]

As Ogneva points out, the number of tools and the overall market for them is not only large, but it is scattered with no clear winners. This makes choosing what to use potentially even more complex. So, where does a library start?

The simplest place to begin may be with gauging the extent of your library's social media work. If your library is simply maintaining presences and engaging in conversations via a few social networks, then there may not be a need for monitoring tools that can do everything but clean the kitchen sink. The same can be said for the library that is just looking to track mentions of it online. Something that does simple keyword monitoring may be enough. Free tools such as Twitter Search (http://search.twitter.com), IceRocket (www.icerocket.com), or SocialMention (www.socialmention.com) are essential and basic applications for any kind of online reputation management. For the vast majority of libraries, these are enough to satisfy their need to know or not whether they've been mentioned in the social media sphere.

On the other hand, if your library has a public relations professional on staff and is running various organized online promotions or campaigns throughout the year, in addition to social media engagement, your library may require something that can do more. In these cases, if a budget is available, it may be beneficial to subscribe to a service that can provide more comprehensive tracking and metrics. Additionally, if volume of mentions or tracked keywords rises beyond an amount that your library's staff can handle monitoring with simpler tools, this kind of paid solution may ensure against missing important references to your library.

BOTTOM LINE Tools for monitoring social media are many, varied, and always changing. Be clear about what your library's needs are, and the scope and volume of monitoring required when choosing monitoring tools or services.

AT THE VERY LEAST, GET ALERTED

Regardless of budget, there is one free tool that every library should use. Google Alerts (www.google.com/alerts) automatically sends e-mail updates to an e-mail account when new mentions of specified keywords become known to Google. Alternatively, alerts can be an RSS feed, rather than an e-mail message.

Alerts can be created with options to have them sent once a day, once per week, or even "as they happen" (which is perhaps more accurately when they are actually indexed by Google). E-mails or feeds can be up to twenty results or as high as fifty. Alerts can also be modified to search specifically for video, discussions, blogs, news, or all four content types.

Your library should at least set up a Google Alert for each of the following keywords:

- The library's full name
- Any variations of the library's name
- The name of the library director
- Names of library board members

You may also find it helpful to create an alert for the name of the county your library is situated in and the word *library*. This may catch other references if your library is not already named after the county it resides in.

BOTTOM LINE ▶ The most basic tool any library should use to monitor social media mentions is Google Alerts. Make sure to set up several, one each for specific names and keywords.

THEY ONLY DO HALF THE JOB

Despite the ongoing increases in technical sophistication, all social media tools, whether they be free or paid services, have a critical flaw. Jason Falls, in his blog post, "Where Social Media Monitoring Services Fail," describes it:

> They're computer algorithms and search spiders that collect infor-
> mation and put it together in a place where you can find it. Some
> of them do a decent job of organizing and stacking and sorting all
> that data so you can hit a button and get a pretty chart or graph,

> too. But none of them do what you want them to do. They only do
> half the job. None of them tell you what to do with the information.[4]

Just like with any other information your library collects, the library will
have to decide what to do with it. Falls also points out: "Social media monitoring is only as good as the decision-maker who does something with the
intelligence."[5] Having and using the tools are only part of an effective plan.
Libraries also need to figure out what the data means.

Many items that are picked up by such tools are ones that need to be
responded to promptly, such as comments and questions. However, libraries also have to view this information through the lens of the long term. The
nature of social media is such that trends come and go rapidly; looking only
at social media in the short term may not be especially beneficial. An effective
social media effort will not only deal with issues as they come up but will also
monitor them for ongoing trends. For instance, does the library usually garner
a significant number of negative comments when it announces a new service?
If this is something that your social media monitoring can plainly demonstrate, the next step might be to figure out how to make such announcements
better, or perhaps the library needs to gather more patron feedback before
premiering new services. In any case, knowing how the library's social media
work is performing over time can lead to truly valuable insights.

BOTTOM LINE ▸   No matter which tool(s) your library decides on, no tool will be able to help
you with figuring out what to do with what it collects. It is up to your library to decide how to
use the data.

WHAT'S THE PLAN?

Once your library begins getting involved in social media and monitoring its
efforts, it will need to know how to respond to different types of comments
and queries, and may also need to prioritize them. All of these decisions need
to be part of your library's social media communications plan. This plan is
likely going to be a different document from the social media policy discussed
in chapter 4. A communications plan can help your library to respond rapidly
and consistently to almost any feedback it receives via social media channels.

For instance, how does your library plan to respond to criticism? Or even to
someone who posts a glowing review of a new service? Some thought needs

to be given to common scenarios that may arise and how the library will react. Some example scenarios to consider would include:

- Negative comments left on the library's website, blog, or social media profiles
- A comment from a patron who thanks the library for service or materials
- An unflattering patron-created video about the library
- A video, created by a library patron, that is positive in spirit but unprofessional in its end result
- An angry blog post by a library patron, decrying the loss of a favorite service or program

It's not only important that the library respond promptly and correctly to these scenarios, it also has to respond consistently. It will not help your library's reputation if, for one situation, the library responds one way and then responds differently the next time something similar occurs.

Having a plan enables your library to invest now to prepare for problems later. Social capital (as discussed in chapter 3) is important, but it is not the same as goodwill. Social capital allows your library to ask for favors; goodwill can help insulate your library from a debilitating public relations fiasco. If your library already has strong patron goodwill built up online, it is more likely to weather potential incidents in the future.

BOTTOM LINE A social media communications plan is not the same as a social media policy. A communications plan instructs library staff how to consistently respond to specified scenarios, while a policy is a set of rules or guidelines about what staff or patrons are allowed or not allowed to do in social media communities.

DEALING WITH NEGATIVITY

One of the most common concerns librarians have about participating in social media is the fear of receiving negative or inappropriate comments on something the library might post. In extreme cases, libraries may refuse to participate at all because of this fear.

The fact is, your library is almost certainly going to get some of these kinds of comments. It is unreasonable to expect to participate in any kind of communication and expect everyone to agree with what you have to say. However, the reality is that these types of responses are far less common than many librarians fear. The Library of Congress made this very clear when they embarked on their highly publicized Flickr Commons project. The project began in January 2008, and by December 2008 it had more than 75,000 user-created comments and tags on its photo stream. Of those, only twenty-five instances were deemed inappropriate—less than 1 percent.[6] In addition, posting photographs to the social photo-sharing site increased hits to the website of the Library of Congress, and the number of views of many galleries, in some cases, were as much as 60 percent higher than they had been the year previous to the project.[7] Plainly, Flickr Commons was a winning venture for the Library of Congress, and the library was not fazed by the very small number of problematic or negative responses.

It's not comfortable when someone pans your library, and librarians can get very upset when attacks are made via social media. However, it's essential to remember that these negative feelings from patrons have always existed; the only difference is that social media can magnify them and does so in a public forum. In his blog post, "You're Pissed Off at the Wrong Guy," social media consultant Jay Baer writes:

> . . . the ire you direct at the customer that DARED to slam you in a blog comment is wholly misplaced. The customers that take you to task in social media aren't the ones you need to worry about. It's the customers that don't care enough to even complain—or have forgotten you entirely—that are truly dangerous to your corporate well-being.[8]

Baer points out that organizations spend too much time worrying about the negatives in social media and not enough about finding ways to engage those customers who don't care about them. There are far more people who don't interact that your library can be concerned with than there are people who feel negatively about it. When budgets and political circumstances become issues for a library, it is not necessarily the Complaining Charlies who are the biggest problem; it's those patrons who don't care or don't even know the library exists.

This doesn't mean that negative comments or reviews don't matter, they do; rather, it is a call to organizations to understand that they cannot spend more time worrying about potential or actual comments than thinking about the possible benefits of online engagement.

BOTTOM LINE ▸ Your library is assuredly going to receive some negative feedback. That is not an excuse for not participating. Rather, it is an opportunity to interact with and potentially make a better relationship with a patron. Remember that there will always be more people who show little interest in the library than there are those who actively dislike it.

YOU'VE FOUND A NEGATIVE REVIEW: NOW WHAT?

If your library is typical, it won't see negative feedback very often. But what should it do when it does?

The first step is to figure out exactly what kind of feedback it is. While the fact that it is negative may be blatantly obvious, it will likely take some additional analysis to pin down exactly what the goal of the person making the comment was. Knowing what type of negative comment you're dealing with will make the job of responding significantly easier.

Negative feedback generally can be categorized in four categories:[9]

- *Straight problem.* A patron has an issue with something the library has done and has detailed what went wrong. For example, a circulation clerk was rude or not helpful when asked for assistance. Although it can be discomforting to hear this kind of feedback, it can be truly useful in identifying real problems in your library. This kind of feedback is usually the simplest to identify and respond to.
- *Constructive criticism.* This is much like a straight problem comment, except that the patron also includes a possible solution. Perhaps the rude circulation clerk in the prior example could not only have been more polite, but he or she could have referred the patron to someone else who had more information. It is not unusual for many people in social media to use it to make suggestions to companies and organizations for improvement. This kind of feedback is often less hurtful than some of the other kinds, and certainly more helpful.
- *Merited attack.* Your library did something wrong, and as a result a patron is angry. The attack itself may be very negative or out of proportion to the incident that prompted it, but the underlying issue

is legitimate. For example, consider a comment like "This library sucks! Even when I asked for help at the desk, I was snapped at and didn't get anything I needed." A clear attack on the library, but it highlights what may be a real issue that needs to be addressed.

- *Trolling.* The essential difference between a merited attack and an instance of trolling is that the patron lacks a valid reason to make the attack. The typical goal of this kind of commenter is simply to garner some kind of response, much like a child seeking a response from an adult via inappropriate behavior. Comments like "Get rid of all the libraries—who needs them now that we have Google?" fall into this category.

Once you've diagnosed which kind of feedback you're dealing with, the next step is to determine how to respond to it. Dealing with online feedback is a controversial subject, with no shortage of experts to provide their opinions. It can also be upsetting and even depressing to deal with negativity aimed at your library. This is why a communications plan for social media is critical: it can help take at least some of the thought and emotion out of handling discomfiting feedback.

Often, the first thought of response is made amidst a reaction of shock, anger, or defensiveness.[10] None of these emotions lends itself to creating effective replies. It's vital to put such feelings aside and real thought into how your library will react. If you respond in the heat of anger or with your defenses up, it will likely only serve to worsen the situation rather than defuse it.

There are some broad factors to consider before composing a response to negative social media feedback. Alyssa Gregory, the owner of Avertua, LLC, a full-service virtual assistant firm, suggests some things to mull over before responding to any negative statements.

First of all, Gregory says that one needs to consider the consistency of the feedback. It's not efficient or even ideal to make changes based on the complaints of one squeaky wheel. If one person complains about your library's website, your library shouldn't rush out to redesign it. On the other hand, if the library receives multiple negative comments about the same issue, it's time to examine the website for usability problems. "So if feedback is consistent across multiple sources, you'd probably do well to consider that you're being told the truth," Gregory points out.[11]

Another question to ask about the feedback is, How realistic is it? It's not always practical to make requested changes. There may be feedback that you just can't use, no matter how constructive it might be. Several people may have complained about the new self-check machines being difficult to use, and asked for a return to using people for checkout, but the reality is that the library is unlikely to get rid of the new machines and return to having all books checked out by circulation staff. In this type of instance, your library may need to look at other ways to mitigate patron difficulties.

No one can please everyone—not even libraries. Working with customer feedback requires libraries to inherently prioritize some things over others. It's rarely an enjoyable process, but it's an important one. Gregory concludes: "It often comes in a package that even the most thick-skinned of us would cry over. But feedback is to business what food is to the body. Without it, you just can't grow. The key is knowing what and how to consume."[12]

BOTTOM LINE ▸ Knowing the kind of negative feedback expressed in a comment will help your library deal with it. Never react from a personal, emotional standpoint, particularly one of anger or defensiveness. Negative feedback is essential to your library's growth, regardless of how painful it might be to hear.

BASIC GUIDELINES FOR HANDLING NEGATIVE COMMENTS

Following are some common guidelines for responding (or not responding) to negative feedback. (These guidelines apply primarily to straight problems, constructive criticism, and merited attacks; trolling is a very different type of feedback and will be covered in a later section.)

- *Don't bury your head in the sand.* Sometimes, it may seem simpler to simply ignore a negative comment rather than to deal with it; after all, it's just one person, right? Organizations that use this tactic can often find themselves in uncomfortable quarters. The same power to spread a message quickly that libraries can use to their advantage can be used by discontented patrons to do just the opposite. As was demonstrated by the Save Ohio Library campaign in 2009, just a few active, influential users of social media can spread a message rapidly to hundreds or even thousands of people.
- *Quick response time matters.* Remember that no matter what kind of negative feedback you receive, your library will need to react promptly. Waiting to respond will only serve to make the situation worse, as was demonstrated by the #AmazonFAIL public relations

crisis discussed earlier. Sometimes, just knowing that someone is listening to the complaint is enough to make the disgruntled patron feel better. Ben McConnell concluded that if the Amazon fiasco has taught social media users anything, "it's that your crisis communication plan should include responding within *minutes* on Twitter, if even if to say 'Yes, we're aware of the situation.' That won't necessarily neutralize a bad situation, but it will demonstrate a company that's keeping up with the times. When opinions are being influenced by a digital-driven word of mouth, that's worth a lot."[13]

- *Be the first, and don't let others speak for you.* This is another reason that a fast reply is critical. In order to maintain the credibility and reputation of your library, make sure that people hear what happened from you, not from others. When nothing authoritative is said, people will speculate, often veering toward the negative. Even if what your library has to say isn't something that will make people happy, it's imperative that the message come from the library and quickly. Patrons will lose trust in short order and assume that the library is trying to sidestep an issue, much like what happened with Amazon.com. "Credibility is the currency of the new normal," Steve Cody, managing partner and cofounder of Peppercom, says.[14] Even if your library is not trying to avoid something controversial, simply delaying the response can cause speculation to run riot and give the appearance of doing so.

- *Saying "We don't know" is OK.* Some libraries believe that they have to have everything perfect and in place before they can respond to a complaint. This can contribute to delays and, in turn, worsen a social media exchange. It is far better to reply right away with "We don't know the answer, but we'll find out and get back to you soon as we can," than to either delay until the answer is known or reply with something unlikely to satisfy the complainant. Often, people who make negative comments simply want to be heard, even if they can't get the problem resolved right away. A vague answer is only more likely to anger the complaining patron further.

- *A tweet may not be enough.* If a complaint comes in via Twitter, it may seem natural to want to respond through the same medium. However, rarely are 140 characters (the limit for Twitter) going to be enough to offer a thorough response. As tempting as it might be to shoot off a quick message and be done with it, your library is better off using Twitter to ask the patron for an e-mail address and quickly explain that it will be able to better respond at more length that way. Also, by allowing for more direct and lengthy communication, you may uncover relevant details that were not available previously. If your library and the patron work it out, outside of the medium that the complaint originally complained in, be sure to add a post or tweet clarifying that the situation is resolved and how it was resolved. Otherwise, people who were watching that subject thread may believe that the comment was ignored entirely.

- *Tone matters.* Sounding formal in social media is generally considered inappropriate. Add that stiff formality to a reply to a patron complaint, and it can quickly turn a small complaint into a larger one. Remember that people want a person to talk to, not an organization. In many cases, the patron wants empathy more than anything else. A human voice can go a long way toward defusing a tense exchange of communications.

- *Don't be defensive.* As difficult as this might be, it is perhaps the most important rule for dealing with unhappy patrons, online or offline. Your library needs to be willing to accept responsibility for problems, and sometimes that means admitting that there was, in fact, a problem, and thanking someone for bringing it to your attention. Excuses will only make the complainant more hostile. Remain calm, despite any provocation. Listen before allowing your library to react. Lisa Barone, the cofounder of Outspoken Media, put it very bluntly:

> If you can't remain calm in a fight, then you should not be allowed to participate in social media. The moment you lose your cool, you've not only lost the discussion, you've also just thrown 20 gallons of kerosene into the blaze. Good luck making amends with anyone once you've shown that you don't take criticism well and that you haven't yet mastered how to play well with others. Oh yeah, and it almost always makes you look like a jackass.[15]

- *Take responsibility.* Apologize right out of the gate for any mistake that your library may have made. Even if your library wasn't the culprit, show sympathy for the problem of the patron. Be clear about how the problem happened, but do not attempt to put the blame on anyone or anything else. Attempting to shift blame or making personal attacks on the other party only serves to make the library look unprofessional. Pointing fingers solves nothing and will almost certainly inflame the situation. If there is nothing your library can do to solve the problem, such as when a policy decision has been made that the patron dislikes, still thank the person for the feedback and explain why the decision was made.

- *Make a public promise.* Whatever your library's reply, be sure to end it with how the library will do better in the future. What will your library do to be sure this doesn't happen again? How will it make amends to the unhappy person? It's important to not only figure out the answers to these questions but also to post your answers publicly. Private replies may make the dissatisfied patron feel better, but they will do nothing to quell the curiosity of people following the scenario online. If the resolution is not available to the public at large, it is likely that the public will simply conclude that the situation was not handled by the library or it was disregarded altogether. This is also a very important opportunity to show your online community that the library is an engaged, transparent organization.

BOTTOM LINE Your library's response to negative feedback represents a prime opportunity to show that it is operating as it should in social media. Drop the defenses, apologize, and rectify the situation—in public.

WHAT IF IT'S A TROLL?

There is a common saying online: "Don't feed the trolls!" If you have determined that a comment is the work of a troll, rather than something legitimate, your best response is actually no response at all. This kind of post is almost always an attempt to bait your library into a pointless argument. The goal of the troll is simply to provoke a response—*any* response (see figure 8.2).

Some people simply are looking for a fight. They only want to incite arguments or make the library look bad, rather than to actually discuss any issue. The more participants who engage with these kinds of people, the more likely it is to drive the troll to further efforts for attention, maybe even the loss of control by the library over, for example, its Facebook Page. Such types can also ruin an online space by causing others to simply leave in order to avoid the controversy.

Note that the best strategy is to ignore the trolls, *not* to delete what they post. Deleting posts may only egg the troll on, causing him or her to redouble efforts to be seen. However, if you find that this person is using hateful or

Why I Troll
By Trolling4Dollars, a well-known troll on Slashdot.org

Before the web changed reading and writing (for better and for worse), people used to be held captive to the words of only a few. These people were experts, specialists or authorities of varying degree, or the occasional lucky soul whose writing won the lottery of the editorial columns in papers and magazines. This was how we discussed ideas and exchanged information before the Internet gave everyone the ability to write; more importantly, before everyone could have his/her writing seen by others in public venues. Many times, in those days long past, one would read something that was presented as the final say on some topic. If you were someone who had more knowledge about that topic, you would be quite annoyed, and later extremely frustrated, that there was little chance for rebuttal.

In the early days of my experiences on the Internet, I would find many comments on subjects I knew which were patently wrong. Not the sort of wrong that usually begins with an "I think", or "It seems to me", but the sort of wrong where 2+2=5 or where nuclear is pronounced: "nook-you-lar". Knowing full well that people don't appreciate being corrected, I knew that the usual methods of notifying these mistaken individuals of their errors would fail. Instead, I embarked on more subtle means of having others point out the flaws in their thinking. Thus, my entry into the world of trolling.

At the core, I'd say that I troll because it's an easier way of motivating people to analyze their positions on a topic. Not only does one of my trolls change the direction of the conversation, but it also pulls other people off the fence who might be thinking the same thing I am but don't feel comfortable being the first to say it. In some cases those people might be trolls too, or they might not. In the long run, the conversation and exchange of ideas is altered and perhaps a little more constructive than if it were left to the supposed experts of the forum where the status quo is left to rule.

Given that most of my trolls were usually in technical forums, there were many times when I'd see assertions made by the forum's "experts" that were completely mistaken. However, few would want to challenge those authorities without being perceived as authorities themselves. This is a difficult status to attain in many circles, but it does not necessarily mean that one's knowledge of the subject is lacking. It simply means that some people are better at presenting their knowledge than others. To me, it's infuriating when someone is deemed an authority and is spreading incorrect information. Many times these were the situations where I would come out from under the bridge. Someone was wrong on the Internet and I sure wasn't going to let that remain so.

Cont.

FIGURE 8.2 **"Why I Troll" manifesto**

The types of trolls on the Internet are as varied as are the personalities of the real people behind them. It's hard to categorize trolls. A more effective method would be to categorize some of the motives behind trolling. This is not an exhaustive list, but these motives are fairly common to many trolls:

- *"I'm right and you need to be corrected"* This kind of troll arises from the need to correct a perceived error in fact. Sometimes these sorts of trolls can bring about useful discussion even if it is off-topic.
- *"I don't care about your sacred cow and I'm going to make hamburger with it to show you why you shouldn't care either. Mmmm tasty"*. Examples of this are threats to burn a symbol that is valuable to one group of people. Book burnings and flag burning, are real life examples of this mind set. When these topics move from real life onto the web, the trolls become more aggressive because there is far less of a threat of negative retaliation than there is in the physical world.
- *"I'm completely off my rocker."* Just as in real life, there are some people on the web who have mental problems and they will post frequent and aggressive rants.
- *"I dislike it when other people are happier than I am, so I'm going to make them miserable."* This motive can sometimes be a subset of the "I'm completely off my rocker" trolls. These are people who just are not happy and want to spread their misery. They are usually damaged people. They have some sort of problem where they either actively enjoy hurting other people, or they are sociopaths who just don't care as long as they have center stage. They're the same people who hurt themselves and people in real life and now they have access to the web.
- *"The Internet is bad and I'll prove it by making it bad."* This person believes that the whole of the internet is a waste of time and sharing information is pointless. The troll, who is probably totally normal in everyday life, goes to great extents to try and "prove" that the internet is "bad" by actively making it bad. I've seen a handful of them, when pressed, admit that they are only mistreating others so that the others will learn that no one is to be trusted. They see this as a valuable lesson. This is just one of the milder variants of the kind of person who enjoys hurting people. They want to take others who they perceive as "naive" and rub their faces in the disturbing and ugly side of the internet (and the world).
- *"Your viewpoint is irrelevant because I can't understand it."* Some trolling is also based on maturity level. When you're, say, a 13 year-old, you just don't understand why a parent would be sensitive to

FIGURE 8.2 **(cont.)**

tasteless jokes about kids. This results in a very different kind of troll.
- *"My agenda is the right one."* On the other hand, when you're a 21 year old male who's read some book that has redefined your life and you think you see the world as it really is, you now have an agenda. And you work hard to make sure everyone knows that you're right. Yet again, a completely different kind of troll results.

One thing that I think many people forget is that when dealing with people on the web, there are real people at the other end. That doesn't just apply to how you treat others, but also in how they will treat *you*. In real life , most people don't expect that they will never meet people who are arrogant, vindictive, opinionated or even dangerous. That should carry over onto the web, too.

racist language, it is a different matter. In these cases, not only should the comment be deleted, but the troll should also be blocked from and reported to the social network it appears on. The rest of your community actively wants a pleasant environment, and dealing with this kind of troll is part of online community management.

BOTTOM LINE ▸ The patrons who connect and converse with you in social media want a good community, not one where the trolls are out of control. Don't feed the trolls. Ever.

WHAT IF THIS IS A REPEAT OFFENDER?

What if ignoring the troll isn't working? Alyssa Gregory provides some concrete advice for dealing with trolls that don't seem to go away:[16]

- *Find out more about them.* If they have a website listed, view it. You can also look at their social media profile and look for clues. If possible, Google them. If they are commenting on your library's blog, check to see if their IP address was recorded. It's important to know if they have a history of trolling in other places, or if it is specific to your library. Check to see if this is habitual or a one-time (or one location) thing. "If you're able to get an idea of what is motivating them to post inappropriately, you can make an informed decision on how to handle the situation," says Gregory.[17]

- *"Kill them with kindness."* Another option is to not allow the library's response to be an angry one, but rather to thank them for the comment and perhaps even compliment them on an aspect of it. This may catch them off-guard, since it will not be the reaction they were seeking. This is a somewhat riskier strategy, as they may still attempt to provoke you.

- *Finally, block and report them.* If they are truly disruptive to your community, or the situation escalates to personal attacks, invasions of privacy, or excessive harassment, it is probably time to ban them from your blog, Facebook wall, and so on. If the problems are occurring on a social media site, it is best to also report them directly to that site, so that administrators have an ongoing record of this person's wrongdoing. By the same token, it's important that your library maintain a log of all the relevant interactions with the troll, especially if your library reports them to another service. Gregory says: "This is a rare but very serious situation, and one you want to be prepared for."[18]

BOTTOM LINE   As much as libraries want to win over everyone, there is the rare person who is not interested in being won over. Be prepared for the worst, even if it's unlikely to happen. Then move on.

NEGATIVE FEEDBACK RESPONSE MAKEOVERS

It may be easier to visualize how your library can respond to negative feedback by looking at both good and bad examples of such responses. In this section, I'll offer some examples of responses that are problematic. I'll also show some ways that these same replies can be remade to be potentially more effective.

Fictional complaint made via Twitter from @disgruntledpatron:

> *"@examplelibrary Why do my books always come in at once? Drives me crazy, and I never get them all read & then I run up overdue fines!"*

Less Effective Response

> *"@disgruntledpatron Try reserving fewer at once. That may help."*

Why Is This Response Ineffective?

First, there is no sympathy for the plight of the person complaining. Remember, people want empathy almost more than they want the problem resolved. Second, there may be other options that would help, such as offering to put holds on books the patron couldn't read, or even helping obtain a digital copy. This response doesn't offer any real help; rather, it puts the burden of solving the problem entirely on the person complaining.

REMADE EXAMPLE ONE

> *"@disgruntledpatron This happens to us, too! Just ask us & we can help you get copies of what you couldn't read (even digital ones) when you're ready!"*

Why Is This Response Better?

It lets the patron know that even the library staff has this same issue and that they are not alone with the problem. The tweet also tells the patron that the library is ready and willing to help and does not attempt to shift the blame for the problem onto the patron for potentially ordering too many titles at once.

Fictional complaint made via Facebook Wall from a patron named Jim:

> *"I thought libraries were supposed to be quiet? The last time I was in your library, there were kids running everywhere (not just in the children's room), and I saw the security guard just standing there doing nothing. My tax dollars at work…NOT!!"*

Less Effective Response

> *"Libraries aren't really like that anymore, unfortunately. We'll let the director know about the security guard."*

Why Is This Response Ineffective?

Again, there is no real sympathy apparent here; empathy for the complaint will almost always help to defuse a patron's anger. Although the response uses the word *unfortunately*, that implies that the library is as dissatisfied as the patron about the state of noise in the library. In many cases, this would not be true. Many libraries pride themselves on being community centers, rather than purely as quiet temples of knowledge. The reply does make a promise to report the security guard, but doesn't really include a promise to follow up with the patron.

"Hi Jim—Thanks for your feedback! We know that the noise level in many libraries nowadays is a surprise to folks who haven't been in one for a while. Libraries have evolved into a different kind of place than when many of us were growing up. Rather than being just a place where librarians shush people all the time, libraries now do so much more! We are often centers of our communities (and noise comes along with that role) as well as places to get books and information. We do provide quiet zones at most of our branches, and often we may also be able to reserve a quiet study room for you. However, you're right—we don't want kids literally running around the library (we have no plans to take up a role as a race track). If you would like, you can e-mail details of the incident to us at contact@examplelibrary.org and we'll follow up with both you and the security guard."

Why Is This Response Better?

Because the complaint was made via Facebook, the library is not restricted to a 140-character response. This means that the library can create a response with a more human tone; no patron wants to talk to an organization, they want to talk to a person! It also means that the library can go into more detail about why some noise is no longer unacceptable at most libraries. The response also provides concrete solutions for the patron, if he or she still needs a quiet place to be at the library. Lastly, it ends with a request for more information to help resolve the situation for the patron.

Another fictional complaint made via Twitter from a patron named Linda:

"Why can't I ever get on a computer?"

Less Effective Response

"Most computers are on a first-come,
first-served basis. Call (555) 555–5555
to reserve one ahead of time."

Why Is This Response Ineffective?

While this response does easily fit into a 140-character tweet, it fails to address a core need. It shows no empathy for the frustrated patron. The last thing an annoyed library user probably wants at this point is a lecture about how the system works, no matter how succinct. When someone uses social media to vent a complaint, they do not even necessarily want to know the reason why something occurred, but may just want a venue for venting their anger. It's essential to address the feelings of the upset person and not just the cause.

REMADE EXAMPLE THREE

"We know it can seem crazy—the
computers get a LOT of use! Try giving
Mary a call at (555) 555–5555 to reserve
one for you ahead of time."

Why Is This Response Better?

First, an empathetic statement is made right off the bat. This may help to alleviate some of Linda's obvious frustration. The statement also shows that the library is aware of the situation and isn't trying to hide it. Remember that transparency lends itself to establishing trust, something that is critical for good library-patron relations. Second, the tone of the tweet is very casual, lending itself to portraying the library as human, rather than as an impersonal institution. The use of the words we and crazy adds to this feeling of humanness, as does the all-caps "LOT." Lastly, to help resolve the situation for the patron, the tweet doesn't give just a phone number, but also gives a name for Linda to call directly. While this is not always possible for a library to do, it does add another human dimension and may help that person feel that there is a direct contact at the library to go to for help.

SOME FINAL THOUGHTS ON ORM

When it comes to reputation management, there is one crucial point at which many organizations go wrong. Many organizations fail to understand basic human nature when it comes to negative commentary. People want to be *heard* more than they necessarily want a *solution*. Much of the time, if people know their opinion has been heard by the library, that may be enough. This is why thanking people for even negative feedback is vital.

It's incredibly tempting to simply delete bad comments so that they never appear on your Facebook wall or blog. However, by leaving them, the library shows that it's authentic and transparent. Libraries need to understand that these kinds of feedback serve as tests: Will the library know how to respond appropriately in the social media sphere? Is the library real and honest enough to converse with a dissident? Can the library deal with criticism under public scrutiny? Will discontents be ignored or engaged? Remember, the online community is watching.

Social media consultant Kyle Lacy sums it up well:

> If all you ever read is good content (about something) then usually you jump to the conclusion that something is not right with that individual. We're not perfect and we can't make everyone happy. The bad comment won't ruin you. It'll give you credibility. It shows that you can take criticism. You can deal with it and you can move on from it.[19]

BOTTOM LINE ▶ Monitor, listen, and then communicate. One (or even a few) bad comments will not hurt your library, especially if handled appropriately. Negative comments are a public test of your library's social media savvy and can determine whether or not someone will want to be involved with it.

NOTES

1. Mark R. Probst, "Amazon Follies," April 12, 2009, http://markprobst.livejournal.com/15293.html.

2. Jackie Huba, "Anatomy of the #AmazonFAIL Protest," *Church of the Customer Blog*, April 13, 2009, www.churchofcustomer.com/2009/04/customers-revolt-over-amazon-gay-book-deranking-aka-amazonfail-.html.

3. Maria Ogneva, "Why You Need to Monitor and Measure Your Brand on Social Media," *Mashable Social Media*, July 29, 2010, http://mashable.com/2010/07/29/monitor-measure-brand-social-media.

4. Jason Falls, "Where Social Media Monitoring Services Fail," *Social Media Today*, April 2, 2009, http://socialmediatoday.com/SMC/186061.

5. Ibid.

6. Jessamyn West, "Library of Congress reports on Flickr project," *librarian.net*, December 14, 2008, www.librarian.net/stax/2607/library-of-congress-reports-on-flickr-project.

7. Ibid.

8. Jay Baer, "You're Pissed Off at the Wrong Guy," *Convince & Convert*, August 4, 2010, www.convinceandconvert.com/social-crm/you-are-pissed-off-at-the-wrong-guy.

9. Josh Catone, "HOW TO: Deal With Negative Feedback in Social Media," *Mashable Social Media*, February 21, 2010, http://mashable.com/2010/02/21/deal-with-negative-feedback.

10. Patricio Robles, "How do you handle feedback?" October 2, 2009, http://econsultancy.com/blog/4705-how-do-you-handle-feedback.

11. Ibid.

12. Ibid.

13. Ben McConnell, "Crisis 101: now measured in minutes," *Church of the Customer Blog*, April 16, 2009, www.churchofcustomer.com/2009/04/crisis-101.html.

14. Abbey Klaassen, "How to Weather a Twitterstorm," *Ad Age Digital*, April 14, 2009, http://adage.com/digital/article?article_id=135991.

15. Lisa Barone, "How Companies Should Respond to Negative Reviews," *Outspoken Media*, April 13, 2009, http://outspokenmedia.com/reputation-management/respond-negative-reviews.

16. Alyssa Gregory, "How to Deal with Trolls on Your Blog," *SitePoint*, November 6, 2009, www.sitepoint.com/how-to-deal-with-trolls.

17. Ibid.

18. Ibid.

19. Kyle Lacy, "Keep Your Friends Close and Your Followers Closer," July 26, 2010, http://kylelacy.com/keep-your-friends-close-and-your-followers-closer.

9

WHAT CAN WE COUNT?

Measuring Success

It's not as simple as counting subscribers, followers, fans, conversation volume, reach, or traffic. While the size of the corporate social graph is a reflection of our participation behavior, it is not symbolic of brand stature, resonance, loyalty, advocacy, nor is it an indicator of business performance.

—BRIAN SOLIS, AUTHOR OF *ENGAGE!*

Evaluation of social media is still a somewhat murky and controversial subject. There is no single, defined standard for measuring engagement. Rather, there are a host of expert opinions, many of which differ. In addition, most of the methodologies are really meant to be used with businesses that can track concrete factors such as sales. There are, however, some things that libraries can and should do. Measuring numbers of fans/followers is certainly one, but it isn't the only one. A library can benefit from investigating both quantitative and qualitative progress, which will likely give a better big-picture view than tracking either outcome alone.

If a library has jumped into social media without really understanding why, its haste becomes apparent when it's time to evaluate progress. If there are no stated goals, there will be no way to measure progress toward them. Libraries first have to know *what they want* from social media before they can determine how effective their efforts have been. Evaluation really begins *before* you measure results.

The first step is to decide your library's social media goals and take a baseline measurement. This allows you to do a comparison during evaluation and later on. Typically, a library should be thinking about the possible effects that have nonfinancial but nonetheless desirable impact. These might include the following:

- Website visitors
- Positive press
- YouTube views
- Blog comments
- Retweets (Twitter)
- Visitors to the physical library
- Positive word of mouth
- Number of friends/fans/followers
- Employment applications
- Social media mentions

Look carefully at your library's goals for its social media work. How else will you measure its success?

For instance, if your library decides that one of its goals is to increase the number of comments on its blogs, figure an average number that a post gets currently. (Most, if not all, blog platforms allow you to track the number of comments on a given post.) If the objective is to get more social media mentions, use a tool like Google Alerts to figure out how often your library is already mentioned in a given time period. (Google Alerts will e-mail you any time a particular keyword is mentioned online.) Once you have a baseline number, you can accurately evaluate later to see what progress (if any) has been made.

BOTTOM LINE You won't know how far your library has come with its social media strategy unless you know where it began. Make sure goals are clear and measurable and baseline measurements are known.

QUANTITATIVE MEASUREMENTS

In the profit sector, evaluation of new programs or products is typically done using ROI, or return on investment. ROI is calculated by subtracting your starting value from your final value, and then dividing that total by the starting value. In other words, if you invest $10 and get back $30, the formula will be (30 – 10)/10; your ROI is double the amount of your initial investment.

When it comes to social media, the problem with ROI is that it was never designed to measure human interactions. Even a business with a product to sell will find that trying to justify social media with ROI is imprecise at best and useless at worst. When discussing libraries, which generally don't have products to sell, ROI becomes even more problematic. As I'll explain later, however, ROI as a tool can still help a library measure social media success.

Quantitative measurements that can be tracked include the number of fans or followers. In addition, a library will likely want to track how many people connect to the library in a given period of time within a particular social network. The number of posts to a Facebook Wall, Twitter mentions, and so on are also worth tracking to determine the amount of activity and engagement.

You've got to measure your library's social media work somehow. Without any kind of measurement, you can't know what your library's ROI on the work is.

MEASURING OPINIONS

Knowing the general "feel" (sentiment analysis) of interactions is also important for gauging how your library is doing in social media. Sentiment or opinion analysis should come into play whenever social media is evaluated. After all, an increase in Twitter mentions does little good if most of those mentions express negative opinions. When doing a measurement, baseline or progressive, it's crucial to know if those measurements constitute positive or negative mentions. This means your library should also be measuring negative effects of social media. If the original goal was to increase the number of blog comments, then knowing how many are positive and how many are negative is going to give you a much better idea of what's going on than just the sum of the comments.

Figuring out a qualitative measurement will require you to take a close look at the original social media goals for your library. If you want to track conversation or engagement, you'll need to establish that baseline measurement mentioned previously. To do this, ask such questions as the following:

- Are we currently part of online conversations about the library/ community?
- How is the library talked about online, compared to other, similar (or nearby) libraries or community organizations?

Once you know those answers, you can work on answering these kinds of questions:

- Have we built better relationships with our patrons?
- Are we participating in conversations where we previously didn't have a voice?
- Have we moved from monologue to meaningful dialogue with patrons?

There are a growing number of automated tools that claim to track online sentiment. These include such well-known pay services as OpenAmplify and Radian6. However, there are some major flaws with these tools, and human communications are more shades of gray than strictly black and white. The results that come from these types of tools may not result in any kind of accurate perspective. These tools also usually fail to account for the inherent level of influence of different people and different online social sites. A Twitter mention by a famous person will not necessarily have more weight than one by a noncelebrity. Human sentiment is very difficult to measure in an automated way. As of the time of this writing, it's probably best for your library to avoid these kinds of services until they become more sophisticated.

When it comes to sentiment analysis, it doesn't really have to be complex. What you're really looking for are trends or correlations. Does your library see an uptick in program attendance after a positive social media mention? Or is there a decline after a negative one? Or any effect at all? Is there an increase in Facebook Wall comments after you post a link to your library's new DVD list, and are they complaints or compliments? This is the kind of analysis that is going to make a difference.

In the end, no matter how adept you might be at online conversation and engagement, it's going to come down to how it ultimately affects your library. The library's administration will need to justify the time and effort spent on social media, just as it has to do with any other endeavor.

BOTTOM LINE ▶ Numbers aren't enough; it's important to know what those numbers really mean. Monitor the conversations happening in your library's networks and recognize the primary nature of those conversations, whether negative or positive.

IS BIGGER BETTER?

Nowadays, challenges are common from one celebrity to another to see who can accumulate the most fans/followers. Perhaps one of the earliest and most well-known of these contests was that of Ashton Kutcher and the CNN network. In early 2009, Kutcher challenged CNN to a race to acquire one million followers on Twitter. Of this competition, Kutcher said: "I found it astonishing that one person can actually have as big of a voice online as what an entire media company can on Twitter."[1] Kutcher ended up not only winning the contest, but he also became the first Twitter user with a million followers.

It's not unusual to see individuals, companies, and organizations attempt to collect friends and followers just for the fun of it or to increase market share or buzz. But in the case of a library, does the size of its online social network mean it has more influence or a bigger potential market for its "product"?

The answer to that question depends on how you define *large*. Maureen Evans, a graduate student and poet, found her definition through personal experience. She joined Twitter in its early days in 2006. She soon had one hundred followers and enjoyed conversing with them regularly. In 2007, Maureen began a new project, tweeting recipes that she had condensed to 140 characters. She soon had more than 3,000 followers. Nevertheless, her network still felt like a small community, with regulars frequently responding to her and each other. It wasn't until her audience grew to over 13,000 that the dynamic began to significantly change. At that point, the conversation stopped. The sense of community disappeared entirely. "It became dead silence," Maureen said of the change.[2] What happened? Maureen didn't have nearly the fan base that Ashton Kutcher had.

Social networking doesn't scale once the network gets too big. Kutcher may have a million followers, but it's highly unlikely that his fans are as engaged as Evans's were early on. It's easier to know everyone and feel comfortable in a small neighborhood than in a large one. Clive Thompson, a writer for *Wired* magazine, says: "Once a group reaches a certain size, each participant starts to feel anonymous again, and the person they're following—who once seemed proximal, like a friend—now seems larger than life and remote."[3]

The community falls apart once it becomes too large. "Too large" will be defined differently by each participating individual, but it can range from several hundred to several thousand. Celebrities like Kutcher are part of a select echelon of social media participants who can maintain extremely large fan bases simply because there isn't likely to be such an expectation of intimacy with followers. In other words, as Thompson points out, there is a value in relative obscurity.

For libraries, this is good news. Typically, a library will be primarily targeting a local audience, meaning that it will automatically have a smaller fan base to pull from. The chances of having hundreds of thousands of followers are unlikely. What libraries will have to aim for, then, is not necessarily a quantity of connections, but quality. A library should really be seeking followers who will share its content, because even a small number of people reposting library content can be effective and can trump a large number of followers who don't. It's all about sharing and networking. Your library following may only have fifty people in it, but if one of those people has several hundred people following them and reposts your content, that content has a greater potential to be seen.

This is one of the reasons many people want their content to go "viral": to spread their content as far as possible. Of course, part of going viral is having content that people want to share. But the other part is having a network willing to share it. Your library may have thousands of followers, but if they don't retweet or repost your content, it's not a whole lot different from having no followers at all.

BOTTOM LINE ▸ Extremely large numbers of social connections don't usually scale into viable online communities. Focus on connecting with people who will share your content, not on acquiring large numbers of fans or followers.

EVALUATION AND REACH

One way to think about the effects of your library's social media efforts is to consider the idea of *reach*. According to Rebecca Atkinson, a freelance web marketer and analyst, reach is made up of three factors:[4]

- *Conversation/mentions.* This refers to reach in the sense of where and how often your library is being talked about. Obviously, the more places and more times your library is being discussed, the better.
- *Sharing.* The reach of your library can also be considered by examining how many times its content is shared. How many people are retweeting or reposting library content?
- *Social media referrals.* Another piece of this is to take a close look at the analytics for your library website. How many visitors to the website come from a social media site?

Reach comprises all three of these factors. Adding them together will give you a fairly accurate picture as to how many people your library is reaching through social media channels. Having a concrete idea about how many people are interacting with your library's content is a good way to begin to measure success.

Once you know how many people your library is reaching, the next step is to figure out just how much social media is costing your library. It's probable that your library invested more time than money on social media over a given period. This means that to really know your actual ROI, you will need to know the cost of the staff time. So, as an example, let's say that one staff member, who makes $20 an hour, spends three hours per week on social media for her library. This sample library has the following reach statistics for the past week:

- Ten separate conversations where the library was mentioned
- Content from/about the library shared fifteen times
- Fifty-eight site visits generated by referrals from social media sites

The total number of people reached this past week was eighty-three. The cost of the efforts to reach these people (staff time) was $60. To get the cost per reach, divide the total of number of people reached by the total cost of the effort. In this case, each reach would cost the library $1.38.

All of this begs the question, Is $1.38 per person a good amount for the library to be spending? This can only clearly be answered by knowing how much actual effect the library's reach has had on the library. This is where you will need to revisit once again the library's goals. Is the library benefiting in some way from these efforts? More patron awareness? More blog comments? More attendees at library programs? Whatever the goal, being able to show a tangible return is really what determines whether or not a social media campaign is successful. Comparing this cost to that of a similar outreach activity such as print marketing may help put it in perspective as well.

Your library's ROI is something that also needs to be looked at over the long term. Some weeks or months will be better than others, but it is the long-term trends that will be especially meaningful. This is particularly important in social media where it's likely your social graph will expand over time. The more connections you have (up to a point), the more potential there may be to spread your message. Over longer periods, this will likely mean that you will see increases in some reach criteria. Also, some library content will be more viral than others, resulting in some periods where you may see an activity spike in factors such as mentions. This is a primary reason for why simply experimenting with a social media account is not likely to bear much fruit. Effective social media requires a steady time investment and a commitment to continue working until you realize your goals. Building a social network is not something that happens overnight.

BOTTOM LINE ▸   Measuring reach may be the route to a solid benchmark of a library's efforts in social media. Keep in mind that this measurement will likely mean the most in the long term.

NOTES

1.   John D. Sutter, "Ashton Kutcher challenges CNN to Twitter popularity contest," *CNN.com*, April 15, 2009, www.cnn.com/2009/TECH/04/15/ashton.cnn.twitter.battle/index.html.

2.   Clive Thompson, "Clive Thompson in Praise of Online Obscurity," *Wired,* January 25, 2010, www.wired.com/magazine/2010/01/st_thompson_obscurity.

3.   Ibid.

4.   Rebecca Atkinson, "Quantify Your Non-Profit's Social Media ROI," November 2008, www.johnhaydon.com/2008/11/quantify-your-social-media-campaigns.

SOCIAL MEDIA
IN THE LONG TERM

And yet, the novelty has to wear off. We have to get back
to work. We have to wipe at least some of the foolish grin
off our face and go back to making something happen.

—CHRIS BROGAN[1]

SOCIAL MEDIA OVERLOAD

When first we begin to engage in social media, the experience can often be heady and exhilarating. We build up our follower counts. We converse with patrons we may not even have known existed. We promote library services in ways that were not possible before. All of these can contribute to an initial excitement with this new medium. But what happens when the early enthusiasm begins to turn to burnout?

Part of social media burnout is fueled, no doubt, by the way we now consume information. The amount of information available to us now is way, way beyond our ability to process it. We already consume more than three times the amount of information that we did fifty years ago.[2] Many people view the constant growth of available data as a disease that must be controlled.

Adam Dachis, a graphic designer and a blogger for Lifehacker, points out that information overload is something we *allow* to happen, not something that just happens.[3] He refers to social media expert and author Clay Shirky's assertion that people don't suffer from information overload; rather, people have a problem with "filter failure."[4] The ways in which people have filtered information in the past don't work with the newer Internet media. Prior to the Internet, third parties often filtered information for us. Book publishers decided whose books became available to the public. TV and radio stations decided what to broadcast. Newspaper and magazine publishers decided what journalists were printed. Their decisions about economics and quality produced a filtering effect on the quantity of available information. On the Internet, there are no such third-party filters being applied. Everything and everyone is available and accessible. Of course, these media also were not "always on" or obtainable on the go. Now, there is not only more information because of the Internet, but it's also much more reachable than the media of previous generations.

"How do I put 100 pages of 'I HATE YOU ALL'
into a 140-character tweet?!"
(Caption by Jamey Fletcher)

Overload itself isn't really a new problem. There has been more information available to humans than they can possibly consume for hundreds of years. Yet, it is only recently in human history that this idea, that too much information can make one ill or stressed, has come into the general consciousness. Social media adds to this idea, as it is much like a constant stream of human consciousness. Even when we're not paying attention, the data being produced never stops. There is no option to manage information production at the source, only downstream.

For libraries and the people who manage a library's online social presence, this issue is compounded. Unlike an individual, there is not a realistic option for a library to step back entirely for several months when exposure to social media becomes too much. Managing the library's online reputation is a job that necessarily requires consistent listening and interaction. If the library's social media coordinator is doing his or her job well, that person will be constantly tuned in to various social media channels and have regular conversations. Coupled with probable expectations from the library's administration concerning desired results, and the path to burnout may seem almost inevitable.

Fortunately, this does not need to be the case. It's important to incorporate some burnout avoidance strategies into the library's overall social media plan. The next section will cover some tactics libraries can use to prevent social media burnout.

BOTTOM LINE ▶ Social media can become overwhelming, especially for library staff who have to pay attention to and engage with it. Be sure to plan for this possibility by including at least some methods for avoiding burnout in the library's comprehensive social media plan.

AVOIDING AND REDUCING SOCIAL MEDIA STRESS

Realistic Goals Are Critical

Planning for realistic results is one of the key components of preventing future stress. If the library's goals are directed at gaining big objectives too quickly, it's a recipe for certain burnout and failure. Expecting to gain hundreds of followers in a few months or to converse with fifty unique fans a quarter may be impracticable, especially for smaller or even mid-sized libraries. If your library's social media coordinator is stressed about not meeting stated goals, the first step is to ensure that those goals were possible to begin with. Remember that social media management is an ongoing process that builds results slowly. "Overnight successes" are as rare online as they are offline.

Aside from being practical about what's actually possible in social media, always be clear about why the library is doing it in the first place. Otherwise, when things aren't looking quite as rosy as they did at the start, you'll be less likely to still see the advantages and opportunities that social media can provide. If you or the administration begins to feel disillusioned, there may also be a feeling that there is no real point to social media. This can lead to a risk of disengaging from social media entirely, and losing valuable potential benefits over the long term. It's better to reassess the approach the library is taking (see "Reasons That Social Media Efforts Fail" later in this chapter). Social media success is something that can only happen with a lot of work. Real, meaningful results only occur over time. Be sure that your library is realistic about how you define success and how long it takes to achieve.

If the library's expectations are unrealistic, either about quantity of results or the results timeline, it will inevitably end with staff stress. Just as with any other kind of technology or tool, social media is not a silver bullet. The benefits of doing social media are almost always and only realized over the long term.

Selectivity Is Your Friend

It's easy to become inundated with the choices of networks available in social media, and new ones seem to pop up almost weekly. These services seem to come and go, as does the hype associated with them. Ning, a social network that allows users to create their own niche social networks around special interests or topics, had a good deal of momentum when it launched in 2005. In 2010, Ning changed its business model and eliminated the ability to create new networks for free, instituting fee-based creator accounts instead. Free accounts were allowed to expire in August of 2010. Suddenly, it was very clear that Ning was exactly what it had always said it was—a network for creating *niche* social networks. While many librarians continued to participate on Ning, it was plain that Ning was not the place where a library's patrons were likely to be found. Even if they were, they would be on Ning to converse with groups with very specific interests that were unlikely to be just chatting asynchronously with their library. While Ning has its strengths, it is probably not the right tool for most libraries. Media writer Georgina Laidlaw points out:

> The fact that a social network exists and targets you doesn't mean you have to join it. Be choosy about the plethora of options. Weigh up the pros and cons of each, and try to get an idea of which ones will give you the greatest return for your time and energy.[5]

This is especially important to consider when it's a library that is in question. Although your library no doubt has patrons with incredibly varied interests, it is simply not possible to try to engage all of them in multiple places online. Libraries, especially public ones, have a tendency to try to be "all things to all people." This philosophy is not only impractical, it's exhausting. Strive to narrow down your library's social media "places" online to only those where you know your patrons are and to a number that your library staff can actually support—and support *well*. If your library can only do Facebook and not Twitter, that's all right. It's better to handle one service well than two badly. A library does not need to join more than a few social networks to do what it needs to do. It's fine to have one or two core networks and to leave the others alone. The ones that are on your library's shortlist are where the library should focus its attention. If your library has the time and staff, perhaps it can expand to some others. But the goal is not to be everywhere online; the goal is to communicate with patrons. Think of it this way: Is it easier to respond to e-mails when they are aggregated into one e-mail account or when they are spread out across several? Social media is the same. The more collated your library's social media efforts, the easier they will be to manage.

People Come and Go

Generally speaking, we want to make our patrons happy. Most of us don't enjoy rejection. It can be demoralizing when your library receives complaints. However, another form of rejection comes with participation in social media when followers, fans, or friends jump ship.

It can be very easy to take unfriending or losing followers to heart. It can lead one to wonder, "What did I do? What did I say?" Taking the loss of an online connection with the library personally can cause stress in library staff, and this kind of stress is unnecessary. Just as the tools for creating relationships with patrons online come and go, there is also often an ephemeral element to those same relationships. People's interests change over time. People move away from your library's service area. There are many, many reasons why people sever online relationships, and it happens all of the time. In the vast majority of cases, you will never learn what caused someone to drop out.

Don't focus on the loss of a single follower, but on trends. Was there a significant drop after a particular tweet or post? Had your account been inactive for several days? Many people weed their followers regularly, and those who appear to have stopped posting are often the first to go. Rather than stopping and bemoaning the loss of a follower or two, keep going. Losing (and gaining) connections is all part of participating in social media and not always a reflection on the work that your library is doing.

BOTTOM LINE ▶ Social media work can be time-consuming and easily can turn into a very stressful effort. Make sure that your library's goals are actually reasonable and that it has pared down its efforts to the most essential social network to avoid staff burnout.

Burnout Has Already Set In: Now What?

Unlike doing social media as an individual, a library staff member probably does not have the option to simply walk away when social media work becomes too much. Social media is part of his or her job responsibilities, not a choice. So, what happens when that person feels fatigued or overwhelmed, yet still needs to go on with the work?

Running Out of Ideas

One thing that often gets to social media staff is the perpetual grind. Karl Staib, a business coach for Work Happy Now, says: "It's the routine that kills the most tweeters. All they do is link back to their blog and they wonder why they aren't meeting cool people and having fun connecting with other tweeters."[6] The same applies to any social network where one posts status updates on a regular basis. Not only will being creative help to prevent burnout, but it can also result in more followers and fans, and more online conversations. If you (or the library's social media coordinator) are less bored, you'll generally be less boring. Try some of these ideas to help add variety to your library's status updates:

- *Ask an unexpected question.* Make the question interesting. Asking people their favorite book likely will inspire little, if any, response. Try asking what TV show they recommend. People often enjoy giving recommendations (thus, the success of reviews on sites like Amazon.com). If you can, follow up with a link to past episodes available on DVD that can be reserved or with your own opinion of that show. Humorous questions are often well received, as they can break up the monotony for everyone. What's the craziest thing they've done to get a book back to the library on time? Share the answers so others can see them and get a chuckle, too. Just remember that not every question will be answered, but don't let that deter you.
- *Share a terrific quote.* Whether it's a serious quote from Ghandi or a funny one from an Adam Sandler movie, quotes are an unending

source of update fodder. Of course, you would never want your library's social media stream to become mainly quotes from other people, but they can make good filler when the creativity brain cells are not firing. It may help to make sure that they are not all book or library-related quotes; that will get old for your library's followers relatively quickly. Mix it up with different tones and topics. Perhaps try something like "Silly Quote Monday" with a quote from Yogi Berra to help cheer people up on what can often be the hardest day of the week.

- *Recommend others to follow or "like."* Every Friday on Twitter, it's likely you'll see at least a few tweets marked with either the #ff or #followalibrarian hashtags. Fridays are unofficially considered "Follow Fridays" on Twitter, and people recommend various members of their follower communities that they think are worth following. By giving favorable mentions to others, your library gains social capital and a brief reprieve from having to come up with more original content. You don't have to limit this kind of post to just Fridays (unless you want to use the #ff hashtag on Twitter). Endorsements of others are a win-win situation and something that your library can do at any time, on any of its social networks.

- *Tell a story.* Did something funny or inspirational happen at the library that you can share? Did a child say something hilarious at the reference desk? Did a patron from another state say that they like your library more than the one they have at home? Remove obvious identifying details, but leave the relevant story parts. Think of these as small human interest pieces that can serve to humanize your library's social media presence. This kind of post may be best for a network like Facebook, where you have a longer character limit to work with. That doesn't mean you can't mention it on Twitter and point people to it on Facebook, however. "You won't believe what our staff found in a returned book. See a pic and get the backstory on our Facebook Page."

- *Retweet/repost.* Can't think of *anything* to post? It's likely that at least one of your fans or followers can. Remember, reposting or retweeting other people's content creates social capital, just be sure to give them the credit. It also gives you ready-made, easy content to help you maintain a regular posting schedule.

- *Reply.* Chances are good that someone your library is connected to has asked a question or told or shared something interesting. Use these posts from others as a springboard for your own posts, and to potentially start a conversation thread.

Multitasking Isn't Working

It's very easy to fall into the trap of trying to do social media while at the reference desk or doing other work-related activities. For some library social media staff, this may (unfortunately) be the only way their administration will allow them to participate in social media for the library. In many cases, multitasking is just a myth. It is usually not possible to give equal attention to two thinking-intensive activities at the same time. While we can seem like we're doing two different things simultaneously, most often we're just shifting our attention back and forth. This can result in neither task being done particularly well and in stressed staff to boot. As "simple" as social media work may seem to a library's administrators (and even to the social media staff themselves), it's not all that simple. Social media is human communication, which is rarely straightforward.

Additionally, your library's patrons, if they are conversing with your library online, are doing so because they want some form of attention. The main reason your library probably became involved in social media is because it wanted to acknowledge and engage these patrons. Is it then fair to only give them whatever can be spared within the duration of another job function? A lack of time to properly respond to people will likely result in unhappy, burned-out staff and annoyed patrons.

It's important to ensure that social media work is appreciated by the higher-ups in your library organization. Certainly, the ROI of your library's efforts is important, but social media is doing more. Heather Mansfield of DIOSA Communications, writes:

> Your boss may not understand the important work you are doing for your organization on Facebook, Twitter, YouTube, etc. They may just think this a fad or that you're the lucky one that gets to be on Facebook during work hours. In reality, you're laying a foundation for what is to come . . . the Mobile Web. Social networking sites are going mobile, and so will your nonprofit in the near future, as well as your donors, your supporters, your volunteers, and your board.[7]

Social media is becoming the launching pad for many not-for-profit organizations to become involved with the increasingly popular mobile Web.
Mansfield also points out that many organizations' web traffic has likely
increased due to social media and the mobile Web. If you are able to track
such a correlation with your analytics, this is important information to share
with administrators.

If your library isn't giving you enough time to do the work of social media
well, it's time to take stock and have a discussion with the administration.
Offer up examples where you couldn't answer a patron adequately or do the
follow-up you believe should have been done. Remind them clearly about the
reasons why the library became involved in social media in the first place. Go
over the goals again. Are those goals actually achievable when your attention
is divided? Suggest revising the goals to be commensurate with the time that is
actually available. If your library was trying to have twenty conversations per
week, that may be too much if the social media librarian only has thirty minutes
per week when he or she is not engaged in something else. If your library's
administrators still won't (or can't) give you enough time to do the work as it
should be done, recommend that your library pull back until they can.

Taking a (Short) Hiatus

For many librarians, when they started out with social media, they found it to
be fun and novel. That novelty usually wears off after a time, especially when
it becomes a job responsibility rather than a voluntary activity. It's true that
your library can't really just stop doing social media once it begins, without
potential long-term consequences. For that reason, it may seem that it is also
impossible to take a break when social media becomes too much. Just as we
all need to take an occasional vacation from our jobs, we may also need a
break from social media.

Ideally, there is more than one person who is competent to handle your
library's social media accounts. This is simply good planning: if one person
leaves or is away, someone else is ready to take over. When you're feeling
overwhelmed or need to use sick days, it's incredibly helpful to have an
understudy who can step in while you recoup. You may be able to trade off
weeks or months, further ensuring that burnout is less of a threat.

In some cases, there may not be a backup person available. What happens
then? There are essentially two options:

- *Schedule your posts ahead of time.* There are many tools that allow you to schedule Twitter, Facebook, and other social network posts in the future, and then they will publish the posts at that time. Two such tools are Tweetdeck (www.tweetdeck.com) and Hootsuite (www.hootsuite.com). Scheduling your posts allows your library to still be active while you take a break.
- *Take an actual (short) break.* Very few organizations are on the social media ball all of the time. If your library stops posting for a few days or a week, it's unlikely that anyone will notice. You may even want to post briefly before your hiatus, saying that you're taking a quick break and giving the date on which you'll be returning to normal posting activities.

BOTTOM LINE Variety in your posts can help prevent burnout, as can allowing dedicated time for social media. Ensure that your administration is supportive and find ways to take a break if the work becomes truly overwhelming.

RESURRECTING YOUR LIBRARY'S SOCIAL MEDIA PRESENCE

Social media engagement can be cyclical. Your library may go many weeks or months where it is totally committed to social media, only to have some other periods where conversations and posts are put on the back burner because of other stresses or obligations. Bad experiences can also lead you or your social media coordinator to pull back or significantly disengage. Whatever the cause, negative encounters can add to feelings of burnout or lead to the library temporarily ceasing social media work.

In situations like these, it can be difficult to remember why the library started in social media in the first place. There may be a vague recollection that social media (at least at first) was fun or entertaining. But once the novelty has worn off, it's easy to just let the library's social media presence wither or become stagnant. How can a library recover from an unintentional break or major decline in posting?

Remember Why

Social media is rarely easy or trouble-free, but it can often be amusing and insightful. For an individual, that may be enough. For a library, there are more important reasons to get over social networking declines or humps. Remember that these include:

- *Providing additional communication channels for patrons.* We know that patrons will ask our libraries questions through the channels that are most convenient for *them,* not necessarily for the library. For many, social media is just another way to get a question answered.
- *Building awareness.* By your library being "out there" in social media, it will likely also add to its community's awareness of what the library does and the services it provides.
- *Listening.* Social media also creates additional ways for people to talk about your library in public forums. It's critical to know how people perceive their library.
- *Building relationships.* Social media allows libraries new ways to create and strengthen patron/library relationships on a one-to-one basis.

Georgina Laidlaw writes: "Social networking isn't a life sentence, and it needn't take up your every waking (or even spare) moment. There are benefits to be gained through being part of social networks that suit you. So why not give social networking another try?"[8]

Recovering from a Slump

Just as it can be difficult to get back in the saddle after any kind of failure, it can be equally hard to jump back into social media work after letting it go for a time. To help you ease back into it, you need some strategies that can prevent you from being overwhelmed:

- *Apologize for the lapse—publicly.* It never hurts to publicly apologize. Remember, your library's online followers have some expectation of content when they commit to following your library. A brief apology of "Sorry, I know we haven't posted for a while, but we're back now!" at least lets people know that you are aware of the lapse and that you know it may have been disappointing for some.
- *Admit the problem.* If possible, post specifically about *why* the lapse occurred. If your library just underwent an ILS migration or lost its social media coordinator, be honest about it. People are usually understanding and, more important, this demonstrates a higher level of transparency that your library's fans are hungry for.

Acknowledging the issue behind the social media downtime will further humanize your library's presence online.

- *Start slowly.* Jumping right back in with both feet will likely just serve to replicate many of the original conditions that may have created the original burnout. If your library was originally posting several times a day, consider paring back some for a time.

- *Reassess.* It's vital that you take a very careful look at what caused the lapse you are attempting to recover from. Otherwise, it's all too easy to head down the same road again. If the lapse was caused by other obligations distracting from social media, is there a way to prevent that in the future? If it was caused by a bad or inflammatory conversation, how could it be handled better next time?

- *Ask for feedback.* Coming back after an interruption in posting is an ideal time to ask your fans and followers directly what kinds of content would most benefit them. People like to be asked their opinion, and this may also be a good way to kick-start some new conversations.

BOTTOM LINE ▸ Social media lapses happen. Don't let falling out of the saddle deter your library from its long-range goals. When recovering from a lapse, be human in your library's responses and stop to reevaluate the current social media strategies.

LONG-TERM SOCIAL MEDIA PLANNING

If your library is feeling fairly comfortable with its involvement in social media and has improved its posting using best practices (see chapter 4), it is ready to progress to some more advanced strategies and to begin thinking about some of the challenges it will be facing in the near future. Once your library has been doing social media work for a while, it's time to start looking at some other issues and items on the social media to-do list.

Embedding Social Media in Library Operations

Developing a social media strategy and policy are only first steps to using social media well in your library. The next stage is to make sure that people know where your library is in social media. The best way to do this is to actively embed social media where your library comes directly in contact with patrons. Matt Rhodes, client services director for Fresh Networks, explains:

"Have you checked us out on Facebook?" As I queued to pay at Abercrombie & Fitch in London over the weekend I kept hearing this phrase over and over again. In fact as everybody paid for their purchases the sales assistants asked them this very same question. Some may have found this annoying, some may have found it forced, and some may have found it distracting. But it is actually a sign that Abercrombie & Fitch is taking its social media strategy seriously. And a great example of just how to embed social media across your customer touchpoints and with all your staff.[9]

Having the circulation desk staff ask this same question as patrons check items out is certainly one way to make sure that people know your library is in the social media space. It's very direct and personal—much like social media itself. As Rhodes acknowledges, this approach may turn some people off, but that should not necessarily discourage an organization from using it. The goal here is to make people aware. It also shows an excellent example of an organization using social media. Abercrombie & Fitch does not view social media as something it does separate from other, regular processes but rather as something it does to complement its operations. More than 1.5 million people like Abercrombie & Fitch on Facebook; clearly, this tactic is working for them.

Rhodes also suggests putting your organization's social media channels on the back of envelopes sent to customers, or on any other piece of media where contact information can be found. Examine each customer touchpoint in your library and think about how social media could be embedded there. Here are some suggestions:

- Place signs on the library's front doors asking people to check in on their favorite geo-location social network (e.g., Foursquare, Facebook Places). Keep an eye out to see who actually does this and then welcome them via that same network as soon as they check in.
- Make sure that links to your library's social media channels appear not just on the library's website, but in any e-mails that are sent by the library. Think about all the different ways your library can e-mail a patron—reserves, overdue and "return soon" notices, and probably more. Each of these represents an opportunity to reach a patron where they already are.

- Put bookmarks in display books. Include a message such as "Like or hate this book? Tell us on Facebook!" Include a direct link to the library's profile.
- The continuing proliferation of smartphones means that many people have constant Internet access at their fingertips, including in the bathroom. If your administration has a sense of humor, this is possibly a good place to gain attention. Consider signs with funny messages on the back of stall doors, such as "Got nothing else to do? Follow us on Twitter!"

All of these kinds of practices show plainly a little-known truth about social media: the best social media campaigns have an offline element to them. Human relationships happen everywhere, and having an element to help people connect to the library in both the offline and online realms is simply common sense. After all, a lot of what libraries do on social media is to ask people to connect to the physical library. Why not ask people in the physical library to connect to the social media version?

Fine-Tune Your Library's Online Identity

When your library originally began participating in social media, it is possible that it may have jumped into several networks somewhat haphazardly. It may be that there wasn't a plan in place at the time, and even if there was, it might be that the profile for one network does not match that of another. One of the most effective things that you can do is to give some serious thought to cleaning up the library's social media profiles across its social media presences. Consistency is extremely important, as it helps people to identify your particular library across social platforms and can also add to a sense of credibility for people who view them.

Take a close look at some of the following to see how consistent they are across your library's various online profiles:

- *The library's name.* If your library's name is "Example Memorial Library," it should be that name absolutely everywhere online. Don't attempt to abbreviate in any way, such as "Example Memorial Lib." It is possible to change your Twitter username.
- *Vanity URLs.* By default, your library gets a vanity URL on Twitter (www.twitter.com/your_username_here). However, this is not the

case on most other social media sites. In most other instances, you need to manually set up a vanity URL. On Facebook, it is especially vital to do this, as the URLs Facebook generates automatically are far from memorable. On Facebook, this involves setting up a username for the page (note that this is a major reason for libraries to have Facebook Pages, not personal profiles). You can find more information about setting up a username (and thus having a vanity URL) at www.facebook.com/help/?page=900. As of this writing, it is not currently possible to change the name of a Facebook Page, so you may be forced to match Twitter or other profiles to that of Facebook. Your library should obtain vanity URLs for each social media site is uses, wherever possible.

- *Profile pictures.* Is your Twitter profile using your library's logo and your Google+ profile using a picture of the library's main building? This kind of obvious visual inconsistency can contribute significantly to patron confusion. In addition, not only should the pictures be the same, your library should always opt for its logo rather than any other picture. Participating in social media is an effort where keeping your library's brand foremost in people's thoughts is paramount. No matter how unique or vintage your library's building is, it is not the same as the library's logo, which inherently stands for the library's brand. A brand is more than just a building (or even the logo)—it encompasses all that your library is and does.

- *Bio.* Each social platform usually gives at least some room for a brief description. This can actually be somewhat different across sites. A LinkedIn profile is necessarily going to be more formal than one on MySpace. Keep consistency in mind, but also tailor the wording of the bio for the audience. While you're working on your library's social media bio/description, be very careful of assuming that your library's mission statement constitutes its biography. Most of the time, these statements are simply empty phrases for the average person and do not contain any unique information that makes your library stand out from any other. While it's easy to just use the library's mission statement as the description, it's also a cop-out for writing something meaningful.

- *Design.* On some social networks, such as Twitter and MySpace, users have the ability to customize the look of their profile page.

If you're using a background image, ensure that the same one is being used across sites. Whenever possible, use the same fonts and font sizes. A coherent color scheme (preferably matched to or complementing your library's logo) should be used. Your library's public relations department may have a style sheet for use in library's publications that will be helpful and also assist in ensuring consistency. If such a guide does not exist, this is something that your library should create. Consistency in branding across media creates a stronger basis for credibility.

- *Voice.* Keeping the tone of your updates similar can be a challenge, but it is worth the effort. "Using the same tone of voice will help keep the cohesion," says Amber Naslund, director of community at Radian6. "It doesn't have to be verbatim but there needs to be a certain level of consistency," Naslund says. "You're assuming that [one particular social site] might be the only place they get that [information]."[10]

Planning a Posting Strategy

If you have read this far, you may believe that social media participation for your library could be a full-time job. This need not be the case! Part of your library's ongoing social media plan should also include specifications about how often your library will post. While social media done well necessitates at least a daily effort, it need not occupy more than a small amount of time each day. You can always spend a lot of time on social media, but the law of diminishing returns does apply. The initial amount of time spent on social media daily will usually provide the most benefit.

One way to ensure that this actually happens is to plan, in advance, what kinds of posts will happen when. Try using a calendar or an online task management application such as Remember the Milk (www.rememberthemilk.com) to figure out what will be posted each day. If you know a big event is coming up, plan to have posts before the event showcasing the preparations. Once the event is over, be sure to schedule posts that include photos and stories from the event. When there are not time-sensitive items, have items in reserve such as interesting quotes, articles, or blogs that you will post. Developing a content schedule will save you time down the road and help to prevent lapses in consistency, either in actual posting activity or in types of content posted.

Some libraries choose to devote individual days of the week to a particular kind of content. One library that does this is Columbus Metropolitan Library in Columbus, Ohio. Each Wednesday, the bulk of its Twitter posting is devoted to a practice they call "Who Knew Wednesday." On this day, the library shares a unique and fascinating bit of trivia, usually with a link to a third-party site that includes related information. A tactic like this is very easy to implement and the amount of potential content is infinite, which means the library will never have to look far for items to post about on Wednesdays.

Time management is essential for effective social media. Social media expert Chris Brogan recommends that any schedule for social media be broken up into the following segments:[11]

- *One-quarter for listening.* It has already been stressed throughout this book that social media for a library cannot be just the library promoting itself. Brogan suggests starting your social media work for the day by listening and learning what others are saying to and about your library. This will also potentially give you opportunities to respond to interesting content or to repost something you think others will find intriguing.
- *One-half for commenting and communicating.* This is the time where you actually respond to or repost content. This also includes time welcoming new followers or fans and reciprocating the fan/follower whenever possible.
- *One-quarter for creating.* It takes time to create original content, whether it's blogging, videos, audio, or the myriad forms online content can take. Anything you're building to contribute to the online space should happen during this time. Remember, it is this original content that helps your library connect the most. Search engines love new material, as do your current social media connections. New content can also help you get found online.

BOTTOM LINE ▸ Wherever or whenever the library comes directly in contact with a patron is an opportunity to embed a social media touchpoint. Consistency across social media profiles is critical for real effectiveness. Make sure your library includes posting strategies as part of its social media plan so it does not struggle later with "What do we do now?"

CHALLENGES IN SOCIAL MEDIA

As your library progresses in the social media sphere, it will probably find itself facing trials it hadn't anticipated. Some issues may seem trivial or not applicable until your library has spent more time engaging online. These problems are hardly unique to libraries; they affect nearly all organizations that participate in social media. How each organization handles them may be different, and there is rarely a single solution that will be perfect for all. Following are some of the major obstacles most organizations face in social media:

- *Transparency.* When it comes to social media, there is lot of talk about the need for organizational transparency, but it can be difficult to actually pull off. Drew Olanoff, a well-known online community manager, strongly recommends a two-pronged approach, addressing both internal and external transparency. Internally, it is important to make sure that all of the employees know what is being said externally. A library should start by making sure that all employees are familiar with the social media channels being used, and encourage them to follow those channels. To make the library's social media even more accessible, you may want to consider reprinting the library's content in its internal newsletter or intranet. Social media may be the job of the library's PR department, but it needs to be very open to the rest of the staff. Externally, Olanoff says, "You have to be straight up. If your company fails, you have to be the first to call yourself on it. If you succeed, you have to message that in a way to get people's attention."[12] Transparency is critical to effective social media. Otherwise, your library becomes yet another organization shouting for attention in a way-too-crowded playing field.
- *Relationships.* Perhaps the biggest challenge for many organizations in social media is the switch from thinking of social media as a promotional tool to thinking of it more as a type of customer relations management (CRM). Social media is primarily about individual relationships with online patrons. Libraries that fail to make this change in approach will almost assuredly fail in social media: social media communities will pay little or no attention to those organizations simply looking for attention. It is more important to look for opportunities to build those relationships than

it is to simply accomplish one-time tasks, such as gathering more attendees for a particular program. Focus on those opportunities where you can deepen one-to-one relationships, such as responding to comments and helping to keep an online conversation going.

- *The future.* Another change in thinking that is challenging for libraries is the need to understand that social media is about *long-term* benefits. Social media is about planning ahead and gathering social capital. In order to do this, libraries have to not only listen and respond to their communities, but they also need an administration that supports transparency and is committed to doing social media effectively. Brian Solis, a digital analyst, sociologist, and futurist as well as the author *Engage!*, sums it up: "This is not about competing for the moment. This is about competing for relevance and resonance for the long term."[13]

BOTTOM LINE   Doing social media well will probably require significant changes in your library's culture. Social media work is much more about long-range relationship management and preparing for the future than about short-term goals such as program attendance.

Signs That You Aren't Following Your Library's Social Media Plan

All of the social media work your library does should be a reflection of its social media plan. But after your library has been around the social media block for a while, it may fall into a regular pattern of simply posting and responding. Or perhaps it begins to concentrate on some networks more than others. Maybe it lapses completely for a while. All of these events should prompt you to take another look at the plan. Following are some other symptoms that should prompt you to reexamine the plan and how your library is (or isn't) following it:

Doing social media work can be like climbing a mountain, with the goals far out of sight.

- *Neglect.* The most obvious symptom is noticing your Facebook Page hasn't had any new activity for several days (or, heaven forbid, several weeks or longer). People connect to your library online with an expectation of communication. You need to offer them regular incentive to engage, such as new content. It's time to make sure you have a regular posting strategy.
- *Ignorance of progress on stated goals.* At any given time, you should be prepared to give your library's administration a clear answer to the question, How is our social media campaign going? The answer needs to be something measurable, related to the original goals in the social media plan. Telling your director that things are going well does not constitute a tangible answer. Do you know where your metrics are?
- *Automated posts.* Lisa Barone is cofounder and chief branding officer of Outspoken Media, Inc. Barone says that automating social media is worse than not doing it at all.

> You write a blog post offering a roundup of what everyone else has said about a topic. When you hit publish it's immediately tweeted, immediately sent to Facebook and immediately posted on LinkedIn. When someone follows you on Twitter, you immediately follow them back. When they mention your company name, you immediately retweet it. You may think this means you're living up to your end of the bargain, but you'd be wrong. In this case, you're not doing social media, you're automating social media. In my book, it's worse.[14]

Tools such as autoresponders are impersonal, the exact opposite of what your library should be striving to achieve in social media. As tempting as these kinds of tools might be, ditch canned messages and automated social media tools. Better to say nothing at all than to give the impression that your library didn't care enough to respond with something individualized.

- *Waiting for an audience before posting anything.* This results from misguided thinking about social media. Waiting to post content until after gaining a specified number of connections (e.g., "We won't start posting until we have 150 followers on Twitter") is backwards. People respond to content. Post new content, then you gain more connections, not the other way around.

BOTTOM LINE ▶ Your library spent valuable time on a social media plan. Don't ignore it, and be sure to revisit it frequently to make sure that your actual social media work is on track.

Backing Up Social Media Profiles

As you already know, social media tools are, at best, ephemeral. There is no guarantee that your library's favorite one will even be in existence in a year or two. While this fact is disconcerting enough, it also begs the question, What happens to all of the posts/pictures/video/etc. that my library posted? Over time, you will have created a good deal of original content that your library probably does not want to lose.

The good news is that there is a way to download your content from nearly every social media site. Some have this capability built right in, while for others, you may have to use a third-party site or application. In almost all cases, the process is fairly straightforward. The bad news is, however, that you will need to make a conscious effort to do this; in few, if any, cases, the ability to have data downloaded automatically at a scheduled time does not yet exist.

Your library should plan to make regular backups of its social media data, just as it does for any other kind of data, such as the library's website or a local obituary database it might maintain. Even if your library's chosen social media services are in no danger of going under, having a backup is always a good idea. After all, it *is* your library's intellectual property, and the library should own a copy of it. Additionally, you never know when a particular site might experience a temporary outage just when you wanted to go in there to check something you posted previously. Backups are a smart idea that provide peace of mind in a potentially unstable environment.

What follows is a (very!) brief guide to making backups from two of the most popular social media sites: Facebook and Twitter. Remember that sites can change specific options and settings, so you may need to make adjustments if changes have been made.

Facebook

While Facebook provides a method for downloading a copy of most of a profile's data, it does not provide the same function for pages. This is a problem, but it can be overcome by some third-party services. One of the best-known services is Backupify (www.backupify.com). While it does have pricing plans, Backupify has a free option for three accounts or fewer. The free plan has a 1 gigabyte storage limit and can back up your pages weekly. If your library has more than one Facebook Page, you will need to set each to be backed up by Backupify. Backupify also provides a very long list of available options for each page, so you can be quite selective about which elements of a page are saved.

Backupify also allows for backups from other services, such as Twitter, Flickr, Picasa, LinkedIn, Blogger, and Zoho. It can also save Facebook profiles. Remember, however, that free accounts only allow for three accounts. If your library has more than one Facebook Page, each page will count as one account. You will need to move to a paid plan for more than three accounts.

Twitter

Twitter does not have a built-in mechanism for downloading all of your tweets. As a result, a large number of third-party applications have sprung up to do this. Some are web-based, while others are actual deskop applications that you download to your computer and install. The features of each can vary widely and can change often.

If you're not interested in exploring the backup options for Twitter, I recommend trying TweetBackup, a service of Backupify. Although it can only back up the most recent 3,200 tweets (because the Twitter API service does not allow for more), it does include a list of all the people your Twitter account follows. It can take up to forty-eight hours to build your first profile, so you'll need to be patient. The data can be exported as text, HTML, or in CSV (comma separated value) formats.

BOTTOM LINE ▸ Social media sites can be ephemeral or make your library's older content inaccessible. Make regular backups part of your library's social media plan.

EXPECTING FAILURE

In the end, the question your library administrators will ask is, Is it worth it? No one answer will fit every library, because the goals will differ from one library to the next. Expectations of your administrators will also probably differ. Some may consider the value of actual interactions with members of their community to be invaluable regardless of the metrics. Gathering the opinions of people in your library's community and growing a network of potential advocates has its own intrinsic value that might not be adequately measured with numbers. This is why knowing what your goals are ahead of time will help to answer this question: Is social media worth it for our library? If your library is meeting its stated social media–related objectives, then the answer to the question is probably yes.

Jay Baer, a social media strategy consultant and the founder of Convince & Convert, a social media strategy firm, has written about how surprised he is by how many marketing choices are made purely by anecdote, rather than by making a case based on actual data. He refers to this lack as "decision by anecdote."[15] Unfortunately, many libraries are well acquainted with this methodology; many librarians know that it is not uncommon to hear, when proposing a new idea, something along the lines of "We tried that before and it didn't work."

But, "didn't work" is often subjective or totally in the eye of the beholder. If your library did a direct mail campaign where it sent postcards advertising a program to 400 patrons and that resulted in twelve additional attendees, that probably wouldn't be viewed as a failure by most. Undoubtedly, some would view that result badly, not understanding what actually constitutes a good return rate on a direct mail campaign. In social media, which is such a new marketing medium, the water gets even murkier, since no one really knows yet what constitutes a good return on a given type of campaign. So what would be a failure? In this new media sphere, there is not often a clear answer, except in your library's social media goals. If you aren't meeting those goals, that doesn't mean it's time to quit; it means it's time to look for different ways to accomplish them.

Baer's core question is, "Does your organization EXPECT to fail in social media?" If not, it should. Big companies like Amazon.com that have had major and public stumbling blocks in social media know this. When one approach doesn't work, successful organizations change to another. Eventually, they find the one that works for them.

This is a fundamental truth about social media: failure, at least at first, is probably inevitable. This is not a *comfortable* truth. Baer tells us that this is a critical one, however, that needs to be put out there at the onset of any ongoing social media effort. "By not telling your company executives the truth at the onset—that you are likely to fail before you succeed—you run the risk of giving them a handy excuse to pull the plug and say 'We tried that once. It didn't work.'"[16]

BOTTOM LINE   Expect to fail. Tell your library's administration to expect to fail. And, when you do fail, look again at your library's social media plan and figure out new ways to get to those goals.

How Do You Know If You're Actually Failing?

It's incredibly easy to get wrapped up in the initial enthusiasm for social media. At some point, however, reality is going to settle in and you may find that your hopes don't match the reality. Now what? Do you automatically pull the plug?

The first question to ask in this situation is, How do we recognize failure? Just as with everything else concerning social media, the answer to this is not the same for every library. A situation considered to be a failure by one library might be considered a success by another. Again, to know whether or not your library's involvement in social media has been a success will mean coming back to its original objectives and goals.

The first thing to do when deciding if any project has failed is to look at the original parameters given to the project. Were the goals realistic and stated accurately? Was the project planned well? If the intent was for your library to gain hundreds of followers in just a couple of months on a given site, this may be the cause of your discontent: it probably wasn't a realistic deliverable. As we already know, building social networks is a long-term effort that doesn't usually have instant outcomes. If your library's new YouTube video didn't go viral with thousands of views, this shouldn't be a total surprise. Only a very small percentage of the thousands of videos created daily ever make viral status. Make sure that your library's expectations were sensible to begin with.

Reasons That Social Media Efforts Fail

Even if your library's original plan was realistic and had an accurate time frame, your social media endeavors still may not be up to expectations. There are several common problems organizations encounter that can hinder them in the social media space.

Using the Wrong Channel

Did your library create a profile on MySpace, only to learn that most of its patrons use Facebook? Or did the library create its own social network on a tool like Ning, which has a much more niche audience? If you're not seeing the number of social connections you want to have, it's time to go back and do more research. If you haven't already, survey your library's patrons to see what social media sites they use the most. What you find may surprise you. It could be the majority of your patrons aren't even using social media yet, and that social media may not be the best outreach method for your library at this point.

Using the Wrong People

Just because the reference librarian already had a Facebook profile doesn't necessarily mean he understands how to engage patrons or speak for the library in social media. Likewise, just because the PR person knows how to market with print materials doesn't mean she's qualified to handle social media. It takes a certain mind-set and a certain type of expertise to do social media well. It's important to remember that the best person in your library for the job may not be the one you would normally assign to do something like this. Doing social media successfully for your library is not about a staff member's seniority or position, it's about what will work best for the library.

Creating Poor Content

If your library has been making the common mistake of primarily using social media as a marketing platform for its collections and programs, then its content probably lacks interest or relevance to the majority of its followers. One of the things that makes content successful is making sure there is a "hook" to capture readers' attention. Interesting content will generally be humorous, useful, or newsworthy. Take care to ensure that whatever is being posted is not only useful but also entertaining.

Lack of Contact

Part of establishing any relationship is steady contact. Your library needs to post very regularly. If your social media posts only happen a couple of times per week, this is not enough to build on, especially in a medium where twenty-four hours is an exceptionally long amount of time to go without any communication. Ensure you're participating daily at the absolute minimum.

Lack of Trust

In order for your fans to engage with your library online, there has to be an established sense of trust. Trust is built in many ways in social media. While it might seem easy to trust a library, that's not always the case. Make sure your library's social media profiles are filled out completely and that any avatars being displayed are professional and easy to understand. Again, another component of trust is responsiveness. Did your library wait too long to respond to comments or mentions? Or did it fail to respond at all to a compliment or a complaint? Each time a patron has to wait overly long for a response, chances are good that person will decide the library isn't online to engage in conversation and trust is lost.

Lack of Buy-in

In chapter 1, I pointed out how important administrative buy-in is to social media for getting the end results you want. Without buy-in, you may not have enough time and commitment to implement your library's social media effort effectively. Other issues can arise as well, such as misunderstandings about the purpose of social media or what it can accomplish. However, a lack of administrative support is not the only kind of deficiency in this area; a lack of support from other staff can be just as problematic. No social media coordinator wants to hear this kind of comment: Why are we doing that stupid Twitter thing when we have patrons waiting at the reference desk? These uninformed comments from staff can drain any enthusiasm for the project and ultimately undermine its effectiveness. Even if you succeeded in getting the backing of the library's director or board, there needs to be a sufficient sense of ownership from staff members as well. Being able to identify a lack of commitment (or hostility in its various forms) to social media will go a long way toward resolving issues with those who are directly or indirectly contributing to failed objectives.

Inability to Change

Joshua-Michéle Ross is senior vice president of digital strategy with Fleishman Hillard and an O'Reilly Radar blogger. He writes:

> When an organization makes an investment in social media it is a constructive opportunity to consider not only what could go wrong, but why it could go wrong. In other words, what are the valid criticisms that customers and employees might have and what you are willing to do about it. If you aren't willing to consider the former and have no power concerning the latter, social media might not be your best bet.[17]

Ross points out that those organizations that are doing social media well understand that goals and methods will likely change, even incrementally, as part of their participation. If your library is not prepared to accept recommendations for change from third parties, social media is a difficult medium to be in.

Fear

Fear may be the most common obstacle for any organization as it begins to interact in the social media space. Social media is a new venue, and anything new often generates apprehension. Combine fear of the new with the fact that all of the guidelines for interaction and evaluation are also new (making some metrics suspect), and you can end up with the sense that social media is really too new to, well, even try.

Effective social media often means an organization may have to undergo something of a cultural shift, at least in its mind-set. Oft-touted factors such as transparency, authenticity, and honesty are quickly becoming clichés, but the fact is they still matter. The library's online community is going to want to know what's going on at the library, both the good and the bad.

Make an honest assessment about how your library is interacting in social media. Are responses to questions or comments made from a foundation of fear, honesty, or both? Is the library only connecting to others it considers somehow "safe," such as other libraries or organizations? Is the library sticking only to its usual content, such as links to the catalog or programs? If you find that these behaviors are a regular part of the library's social media interactions, it's time to acknowledge they are rooted in fear. Until the library can overcome that fear, it's not likely social media is going to be a productive medium for it.

BOTTOM LINE ▶   You need to revisit your goals first to know if social media isn't working for your library. Make sure that your library isn't having issues with problematic behaviors, people, or content before deciding to pull the plug. Be prepared to be flexible and to listen. Just as the online community is an open forum, giving staff a chance to feel they are part of the process and that you care about their concerns may be enough to blunt criticism and resistance.

WHEN DO YOU PULL THE PLUG?

As with every new program a library undertakes, there is always a chance it may not turn out as expected. Some endeavors succeed, some fail. If you feel social media or a particular social media site has not panned out for your library, here are some steps you should take to ensure you have covered all of your bases.

- *You've removed all misunderstandings, failure behaviors, and impractical expectations.* You've already tweaked your strategies and managed any other issues mentioned previously, so you know your goals are within reason and not being hindered by other factors. Then you tried again over a period of time and evaluated the results one way or the other; in other words, you know you've tried absolutely everything to be successful.

- *You've done the objective evaluation of the library's social media presence and interactions.* The results of your metrics or evaluative questions clearly show that there is little or no ROI despite your best efforts.
- *You may already have a lot of resources invested—make doubly sure it's a failure before deciding to opt out.* Don't let subjective or emotional responses factor into your decision-making process. You also may have built up social capital already that may be difficult to recover at a later time.
- *You've enlisted the aid of others within the scope and parameters of your library's policies without success.* Sometimes, all it takes is one person from outside to notice a crucial element or offer a critical piece of input or idea to help set you on the right track. Remember, establishing your library's presence in social media won't be accomplished without careful planning and the contributions of many people.

BOTTOM LINE ▶ You need to ensure that your library did everything it could to succeed before deciding social media didn't work this time around.

HOW TO PULL THE PLUG

Pulling the plug is part of a natural process. Not every project will succeed; this is a risk of trying something new. Recognize this reality up front and try to avoid becoming too personally attached to the project. Once the decision has been made to stop participating in social media, either partially or wholly, be prepared to follow through.

Probably the most difficult aspect of leaving social media is letting go of the connections you have built up. Your library created a profile and people connected to it with an expectation of regular communication. The question then becomes, How do we just stop communicating with these people who trusted us enough to connect? This is a hard choice to make. Table 10.1 offers some dos and don'ts to make the process a little easier.

BOTTOM LINE ▶ Be firm but honest about explaining the decision to stop participating in a particular social network. Be clear about where the library will be online going forward.

TABLE 10.1 **Pulling-the-plug dos and don'ts**

DO	DON'T
Be honest. Explain what caused the decision to stop tweeting, posting, etc.	Abandon the account and just stop tweeting, posting, etc., with no explanation.
Give people an alternative place to connect with the library. For example, if you're leaving MySpace, give them the link to your Facebook profile.	Tell people to visit the library on its website, if there's no way to actually communicate there beyond a basic contact form. People who connected with your library in one medium (social media) will not likely switch to another that uses only one-way communication.
Accept that not everyone is going to be happy about this. Sympathize and respond to individuals if you can and be ready to explain the decision.	Try to please every squeaky wheel who complains.
Keep the account open (do not confuse an open account with posting on it). Never, ever, give up control of a profile with your library's name on it. Even if it is not in use, it prevents brandjacking.	Close the account entirely, making it possible for someone to take the library's namespace on that social network.
Leave a final message explaining why nothing new is happening with the profile.	Leave the account inactive with no final message to explain why there is no new content.

NOTES

1. Chris Brogan, "When Novelty Wears Off," September 15, 2010, www.chrisbrogan .com/when-novelty-wears-off.
2. Adam Dachis, "Why Technology Is So Addictive, and How You Can Avoid Tech Burnout," *Lifehacker,* August 31, 2010, http://lifehacker.com/5625890/why-technology -is-so-addictive-and-how-you-can-avoid-it.
3. Ibid.
4. Gina Trapani, "Information Overload is Filter Failure, Says Shirky." *Lifehacker Australia,* September 22, 2008, www.lifehacker.com.au/2008/09/information_ overload_is_filter_failure_says_shirky-2.
5. Georgina Laidlaw, "How to Avoid Social Network Burnout," *GigaOm Web Worker Daily,* June 1, 2010, http://gigaom.com/collaboration/how-to-avoid-social-network -burnout.
6. Karl Staib, "14 Ways to Fight Twitter Burnout," *TwiTip,* November 20, 2009, www .twitip.com/14-ways-to-fight-twitter-burnout.

7. Heather Mansfield, "10 Tips for Managing Social Media Burnout," *Nonprofit Tech 2.0*, October 22, 2009, http://nonprofitorgs.wordpress.com/2009/10/22/10-tips-for-managing-social-media-burnout.

8. Georgina Laidlaw, "Resurrect Your Social Media Presence," *GigaOm Web Worker Daily*, June 8, 2010, http://gigaom.com/collaboration/resurrect-your-social-media-presence.

9. Matt Rhodes, "Learn from Abercrombie & Fitch: Embed social media in every customer touchpoint," *Fresh Networks*, August 8, 2010, www.freshnetworks.com/blog/2010/08/abercrombie-fitch-social-media-strategy-customer-touchpoints.

10. Zachary Sniderman, "5 Ways to Clean Up Your Social Media Identity," *Mashable Social Media*, July 6, 2010, http://mashable.com/2010/07/06/clean-social-media-identity.

11. Chris Brogan, "How Much Time Should I Spend on Social Media," November 20, 2009, www.chrisbrogan.com/how-much-time-should-i-spend-on-social-media.

12. Jolie O'Dell, "6 Challenges to Managing a Brand on the Social Web," *Mashable Social Media*, June 30, 2010, http://mashable.com/2010/06/30/brands-social-web.

13. Ibid.

14. Lisa Barone, "Creating Your Social Media Plan," *Outspoken Media*, May 19, 2009, http://outspokenmedia.com/social-media/social-media-planning.

15. Jay Baer, "Do You Have the Guts to Expect Social Media Failure," *Convince & Convert*, September 1, 2010, www.convinceandconvert.com/social-media-roi/do-you-have-the-guts-to-expect-social-media-failure.

16. Ibid.

17. Joshua-Michéle Ross, "Why Social Media Isn't for Everyone," *Mashable Social Media*, January 18, 2010, http://mashable.com/2010/01/18/social-media-not-for-everyone.

A FEW
FINAL WORDS

The days of shouting and imposing your
message on the masses are gone.

—ERIK QUALMAN, AUTHOR OF *SOCIALNOMICS*

Social media is a long-term process of building relationships with individuals, rather than any kind of marketing to the masses. This is the core of what makes social media different from traditional media. When your library is tweeting on Twitter, posting Facebook status updates, uploading YouTube videos, or doing whatever comes next in social media, it's all about building those relationships. It's not really about how many followers or fans or views. It's not even so much about branding. It's about creating personalized connections that actually allow dialogue between the library as an institution and its patrons. Regularly conversing with people online can allow them to learn more about the library, and allow the library to learn more about what people want from it.

Social media can allow your library to create goodwill and direct connections, not just within its community, but also to a *wider* community that can get the word out when a crisis might arise (as in the case of the Save Ohio Libraries campaign). Social media is the new, faster, and more widespread word of mouth, and it behooves a library to have a place in these communities and participate in the dialogue. In no small way, it's a lot like the old expression, "If you don't make a decision, one will be made for you." In the case of social media, that decision will likely be made without your consent, knowledge, or input.

What is the bottom line for libraries? At the end of the day, social media is all about *people* and *relationships* with them. To believe otherwise is to waste time and effort. Be human. Spend time listening and talking to others rather than merely pushing out various forms of advertising. Social media is a new way to engage with patrons. Keep that in mind as you go forward and do social media. Do it so it matters.

REAL-LIFE SOCIAL MEDIA ADVICE FROM REAL-LIFE LIBRARY STAFF

I put out a request via my various social media channels, asking for library folks for any pertinent advice they might give to their peers regarding social media. Here is a sampling of what your colleagues have to say to you:

- "Do it. Don't just create a page and let it go on autopilot. Post stuff. Plan stuff. ASSIGN and PAY staff to actually do so." —*Diane Kovacs*
- "Don't plan it & then leave the day-to-day maintenance to an out-of-state firm (yes, really)." —*Cheri Campbell*
- "Using social media is like having a cat. It doesn't stop once you get the cat; you have to feed it every day and take care of it." —*Jim Riordian*
- "Have fun! If you look at it like it is work, you are doing it wrong. If you feel like this is addicting, then you are doing it right!" —*Vincent Riley*
- "Libraries need to accept that their PR departments are no longer in total control of the library's image. Even if a library doesn't actively participate in social media, they should at least be listening to what is being said and act on it." —*Glen Horton*
- "Social media, just as the name implies, is social. No one person or department can tackle it alone successfully. It has to be a group effort. And, oh yeah I almost forgot, not an afterthought to your other endeavors." —*Jim Haprian*
- "Listen, learn, then leverage, as well as . . . collaborate, communicate, connect, and care." —*Greg Hardin*

- "It is definitely work, but too many places see it as a frivolity that ought to be taken care of either while you're eating your lunch, or when you're on your own time." —*Cara Kless*
- "Talk to the kids to find out where they are! A bunch of my kids are on something called Plurk—I may need to create an account there . . ." —*Sarah Amazing*
- "If you're going use social media, make it meaningful. It works best to entice and pique people's curiosity. They want to see photos and videos that have good production value. Refine the writing in your postings. Use plain but interesting language. Leave the library-speak by the side of the road. Spare people the PR dribble. I don't care that your library director met some big shot or that you've won a grant. If you send that to my inbox, I will unfriend you faster than Kim Khardashian goes from wedding to divorce. I can't stress this enough, but never forget that social media is for connecting with your customers and not to kiss your director's tush." —*Ryan Moore*

BIBLIOGRAPHY

Alcantara, Rick. "Who Should 'Control' Social Media within a Company?" *Social Media Today*. March 22, 2010. http://socialmediatoday.com/SMC/183509/.

Atkinson, Rebecca. "Quantify Your Non-Profit's Social Media ROI." November 2008. www.johnhaydon.com/2008/11/quantify-your-social-media-campaigns/.

Baer, Jay. "Digital Sharecropping—Why Most Facebook Customization is Wasted Effort." *Convince & Convert*. October 27, 2010. www.convinceandconvert.com/social-media-marketing/digital-sharecropping-why-most-facebook-customization-is-wasted-effort/.

———. "Do You Have the Guts to Expect Social Media Failure?" *Convince & Convert*. September 1, 2010. www.convinceandconvert.com/social-media-roi/do-you-have-the-guts-to-expect-social-media-failure/.

———. "You're Pissed Off at the Wrong Guy." *Convince & Convert*. August 4, 2010. www.convinceandconvert.com/social-crm/you-are-pissed-off-at-the-wrong-guy/.

Balwani, Samir. "5 Advanced Social Media Marketing Strategies for Small Businesses." *Mashable Social Media*. September 30, 2009. http://mashable.com/2009/09/30/small-business-strategies/.

———. "5 Simple Things Most Social Media Marketers Forget to Do." *SiteFox*. September 29, 2009. http://blog.sitefox.com/5-simple-things-most-social-media-marketers-forget-to-do/.

———. "Don't Rush Into Social Marketing, Think About it First." *SiteFox*. September 23, 2009. http://blog.sitefox.com/dont-rush-into-social-media-marketing/.

Barone, Lisa. "Creating Your Social Media Plan." *Outspoken Media*. May 19, 2009. http://outspokenmedia.com/social-media/social-media-planning/.

———. "How Companies Should Respond to Negative Reviews." *Outspoken Media*. April 13, 2009. http://outspokenmedia.com/reputation-management/respond-negative -reviews.

Bennett, Shea. "Why Everybody Needs a Follow Policy on Twitter." *All Twitter*. July 20, 2009 (9:30 a.m.). www.mediabistro.com/alltwitter/follow-policy_b5263?red=tc.

Blanchard, Olivier. "Olivier Blanchard Basics of Social Media ROI." August 24, 2009. www .slideshare.net/thebrandbuilder/olivier-blanchard-basics-of-social-media-roi.

Blowers, Helen. "Learning 2.0." May 2, 2006. http://plcmcl2-about.blogspot.com/.

Boches, Edward. "Four Mistakes You Could Make in Social Media." *Creativity_Unbound*. September 17, 2009. http://edwardboches.com/four-mistakes-you-could-make-in -social-media.

boyd, danah. "Some Thoughts on Twitter vs. Facebook Status Updates." *Apophenia*. October 25, 2009. www.zephoria.org/thoughts/archives/2009/10/25/some_thoughts_o-3.html.

Brogan, Chris. "Get On the Right Side of the Fence." April 22, 2009. www.chrisbrogan.com/ get-on-the-right-side-of-the-fence/.

———. "How Much Time Should I Spend on Social Media?" November 20, 2009. www .chrisbrogan.com/how-much-time-should-i-spend-on-social-media/.

———. "Prioritize Your Social Media Efforts." November 18, 2009. www.chrisbrogan.com/ prioritize-your-social-media-efforts/.

———. "When Novelty Wears Off." September 15, 2010. www.chrisbrogan.com/when -novelty-wears-off/.

Brown, Bob. "Top reason for Facebook unfriending: Too many useless posts." *Network World*. October 5, 2010. www.networkworld.com/news/2010/100510-facebook -unfriending-colorado.html.

Bullas, Jeff. "Social Media Survey Reveals 92% Of Companies Using Social Media." 2009. jeffbullas.com/2009/11/16/social-media-survey-reveals-92-of-companies-using-social -media/.

Burbary, Ken. "Facebook Demographics Revisited—2011 Statistics." *Web Business by Ken Burbary*. March 7, 2011. www.kenburbary.com/2011/03/facebook-demographics -revisited-2011-statistics-2/.

Burkhardt, Andy. "Seven More Things Libraries Should Tweet." *Information Tyrannosaur*. October 19, 2009. http://andyburkhardt.com/2009/10/19/seven-more-things-libraries -should-tweet/.

Carmichael, Matt. "The Demographics of Social Media." *Ad Age Blogs*. May 16, 2011. http://adage.com/article/adagestat/demographics-facebook-linkedin-myspace -twitter/227569/.

Catone, Josh. "Before You Go Online: Talk to Your Customers Offline." *Mashable Social Media*. November 17, 2009. http://mashable.com/2009/11/17/small-business -customers/.

———. "HOW TO: Deal With Negative Feedback in Social Media." *Mashable Social Media*. February 21, 2010. http://mashable.com/2010/02/21/deal-with-negative-feedback/.

Chartrand, James. "Is Your Website Copy Too Excited?" *Men with Pens*. 2009. http:// menwithpens.ca/no-exclamation-points/.

Collier, Mack. "This is why the 'authority matters' argument is total BS." December 29, 2008 (8:09 p.m.). http://moblogsmoproblems.blogspot.com/2008/12/this-is-why-authority -matters-argument.html.

Connor, Angela. "Six ways to get social media buy-in from the boss." *Online Community Strategist*. November 23, 2008. http://blog.angelaconnor.com/2008/11/23/sixways-to -get-social-media-buy-in-from-the-boss/.

Cottingham, Rob. "Cartoon: Head Count." *ReadWriteWeb*. November 22, 2009. www .readwriteweb.com/archives/cartoon_head_count.php.

Dachis, Adam. "Why Technology is So Addictive, and How You Can Avoid Tech Burnout." *Lifehacker*. August 31, 2010. http://lifehacker.com/5625890/why-technology-is-so -addictive-and-how-you-can-avoid-it.

Doctorow, Cory. "How to say stupid things about social media." *The Guardian*. January 5, 2010. www.guardian.co.uk/technology/2010/jan/05/social-media-cory-doctorow.

Drell, Lauren. "Facebook Timeline: 9 Best Practices for Brands." *Mashable Business*. May 17, 2012. http://mashable.com/2012/05/17/facebook-timeline-brand-tips.

———. "HOW TO: Improve Engagement on Your Brand's Facebook Page [STATS]." *Mashable Social Media*. April 6, 2011. http://mashable.com/2011/04/06/facebook -engagement-data/.

Dvorak, John C. "Nine Ways to Use Twitter." March 23, 2009. www.pcmag.com/ article2/0,2817,2343672,00.asp.

Elliot, Amy-Mae. "What to Consider When Building an In-House Social Media Team." *Mashable Social Media*. November 2, 2010. http://mashable.com/2010/11/02/building -social-media-team.

eMarketer. "Social Network Marketing Expands Sphere." August 31, 2009. www.emarketer .com/Article.aspx?R=1007252.

———. "Why You Need a Strategy for Social Media." February 10, 2010. www.emarketer .com/Article.aspx?R=1007508.

Evans, Meryl K. "32 Ways to Use Facebook for Business." *GigaOm Web Worker Daily*. July 21, 2009 (2:53 p.m.). http://gigaom.com/collaboration/32-ways-to-use-facebook-for -business/.

"Facebook Facts & Figures (history & statistics)." *Website-Monitoring Blog*. March 17, 2010. www.website-monitoring.com/blog/2010/03/17/facebook-facts-and-figures-history -statistics/.

Falls, Jason. "Where Social Media Monitoring Services Fail." *Social Media Today*. April 2, 2009. http://socialmediatoday.com/SMC/186061.

Ferenstein, Greg. "The Science of Building Trust With Social Media." *Mashable Social Media*. February 24, 2010. http://mashable.com/2010/02/24/social-media-trust.

Finn, Greg. "A Portrait Of Who Uses Social Networks In The US (And How Social Media Affects Our Lives)." *Search Engine Land*. June 16, 2011 (12:29 a.m.). http:// searchengineland.com/a-portrait-of-who-uses-social-networks-in-the-u-s-and-how -social-media-affects-our-lives-81653.

———. "What Results Can I Expect From My Social Media Campaign?" *Search Engine Land*. February 3, 2009 (4:00 a.m.). http://searchengineland.com/what-results-can-i-expect -from-my-social-media-campaign-16355.

Fitton, Laura. "Selling Social Media 'Up' to Management." *Pistachio.* October 17, 2008.
http://pistachioconsulting.com/selling-social-media-up-to-management/.

Francois, Laurent. "Sentiment analysis crap in social media." *Social Media Today.* September 3, 2009. www.socialmediatoday.com/SMC/121398.

Fulwiler, Eric. "An 8-Step Plan for Social Media Spring Cleaning." April 1, 2010. www.blog.ericfulwiler.com/social-media/an-8-step-plan-for-social-media-spring-cleaning/.

Gervai, Anna. "Twitter Statistics—Updated Stats for 2011." *Marketing Gum.* July 7, 2011 (1:48 p.m.). www.marketinggum.com/twitter-statistics-2011-updated-stats/.

Gordhamer, Soren. "5 Ways Social Media is Changing Our Daily Lives." *Mashable Social Media.* October 16, 2009. http://mashable.com/2009/10/16/social-media-changing-lives/.

———. "When Do You Use Twitter Versus Facebook?" *Mashable Social Media.* August 1, 2009. http://mashable.com/2009/08/01/facebook-vs-twitter/.

Gregory, Alyssa. "How to Deal with Trolls on Your Blog." *SitePoint.* November 6, 2009. www.sitepoint.com/how-to-deal-with-trolls/.

Hanelly, Andrew. "Five Reasons the Intern Shouldn't Run Social Media." *SpinSucks.* June 16, 2011. www.spinsucks.com/social-media/i-dont-want-to-read-your-interns-blog/.

Haydon, John. "11 ways to promote your Facebook Page outside Facebook." June 11, 2010. www.johnhaydon.com/2010/06/11-ways-promote-facebook-page-facebook/.

Heagney, Meredith. "Teenagers unfriend Facebook for Lent." *The Columbus Dispatch.* February 19, 2010, Home ed., 01A.

Henley, Jon. "Teenagers and technology: 'I'd rather give up my kidney than my phone." *The Guardian.* July 16, 2010. www.guardian.co.uk/lifeandstyle/2010/jul/16/teenagers-mobiles-facebook-social-networking?CMP=twt_iph.

Holson, Laura M. "Tell-All Generation Learns to Keep Things Offline." *New York Times.* May 8, 2010. www.nytimes.com/2010/05/09/fashion/09privacy.html.

Hopkins, Curt. "Facebook's Community Pages Unleashed Upon World." *ReadWriteWeb.* April 19, 2010. www.readwriteweb.com/archives/facebooks_community_pages_unleashed_upon_world.php.

iSpyce. "Facebook Bans 20,000 Kids a Day." March 30, 2011. http://ispyce.com/2011/03/facebook-bans-20000-kids-day.html.

Huba, Jackie. "Anatomy of the #AmazonFAIL Protest." *Church of the Customer Blog.* April 13, 2009. www.churchofcustomer.com/2009/04/customers-revolt-over-amazon-gay-book-deranking-aka-amazonfail-.html.

Hunt, Tara. *The Whuffie Factor: Using the Power of Social Networks to Build Your Business.* New York: Crown Business, 2009.

Johansson, Mike. "10 Newbie Twitter Mistakes Made By Businesses." *Social Media Today.* March 8, 2010. http://socialmediatoday.com/index.php?q=SMC/179967.

Kirsty. "Google+ User Statistics Part II—How Have Demographics Shifted Since G+ Came Out of Beta? [DASHBOARD]." *Bime.* August 19, 2011. http://bimeanalytics.com/blog/google-user-statistics-part-ii/.

KISSmetrics. "Who Likes What? Social Media by Demographic." 2012. http://blog.kissmetrics.com/social-media-by-demographic/?wide=1.

Klaassen, Abbey. "How to Weather a Twitterstorm." *Ad Age Digital*. April 14, 2009. http://adage.com/digital/article?article_id=135991.

Kolakowski, Nicholas. "Facebook Filled with Underage, Unsupervised Users: Consumer Reports." *eWeek.com*. May 10, 2011. www.eweek.com/c/a/Web-Services-Web-20-and-SOA/Facebook-Filled-With-Underage-Supervised-Users-Consumer-Reports-416060/.

Kroski, Ellyssa. "Should Your Library Have a Social Media Policy?" *School Library Journal*. October 1, 2009. www.schoollibraryjournal.com/article/CA6699104.html.

Lacy, Kyle. "5 Ways to Help Face the Fear of Social Media." September 23, 2009. http://kylelacy.com/5-ways-to-help-face-the-fear-of-social-media/.

———. "10 Ways to Build Trust with Social Media." December 2, 2009. http://kylelacy.com/10-ways-to-build-trust-with-social-media/.

———. "Empower Your Employees to Win with Social Media." January 20, 2010. http://kylelacy.com/empower-your-employees-to-win-with-social-media/.

———. "Keep Your Friends Close and Your Followers Closer." July 26, 2010. http://kylelacy.com/keep-your-friends-close-and-your-followers-closer/.

———. *Twitter Marketing for Dummies*. Hoboken, NJ: Wiley Publishing, 2010.

Laidlaw, Georgina. "Get Better Connected on Social Networks." *GigaOm Web Worker Daily*. February 14, 2010 (5:41 a.m.). http://gigaom.com/collaboration/get-better-connected-on-social-networks/.

———. "How to Avoid Social Network Burnout." *GigaOm Web Worker Daily*. June 1, 2010. http://gigaom.com/collaboration/how-to-avoid-social-network-burnout/.

———. "Resurrect Your Social Media Presence." *GigaOm Web Worker Daily*. June 8, 2010. http://gigaom.com/collaboration/resurrect-your-social-media-presence/.

Lauby, Sharlyn. "5 Ways to Make Your Business More Transparent." *Mashable Social Media*. September 30, 2009. http://mashable.com/2009/09/30/business-transparency/.

Lazerow, Michael. "Introducing Our Latest Research: 'Strategies For Effective Facebook Wall Posts: A Statistical Review.'" *Buddy Media*. April 6, 2011. www.buddymedia.com/newsroom/2011/04/introducing-our-latest-research-"strategies-for-effective-facebook-wall-posts-a-statistical-review"/.

Lenhart, Amanda, et al. "Social Media and Young Adults." *Pew Internet*. February 3, 2010. www.pewinternet.org/Reports/2010/Social-Media-and-Young-Adults.aspx.

Lipsman, Andrew. "Google+ Off to a Fast Start with 20 Million Visitors in 21 Days." *comScore Voices*. July 22, 2011. http://blog.comscore.com/2011/07/google-plus_twenty_million_visitors.html.

Low, Roderick. "It's Not the Steps, It's the Connection." *Startup Asia Business*. December 23, 2009. www.techinasia.com/social-media-its-not-the-steps-its-the-connection/.

Lur, Xavier. "If Facebook Were a Country, It Would Be the 3rd Most Populated." *Tech Xav*. March 19, 2010. www.techxav.com/2010/03/19/if-facebook-were-a-country/.

MacManus, Richard. "40% of People 'Friend' Brands on Facebook." *ReadWriteWeb*. November 9, 2009. www.readwriteweb.com/archives/survey_brands_making_big_impact_on_facebook_twitter.php.

Malicoat, Todd. "7 Reasons Your Social Media Marketing Failed (and how to fix it!)." *Stuntdubl.com*. January 12, 2009. www.stuntdubl.com/2009/01/12/social-marketing-failure/.

Mansfield, Heather. "10 Tips for Managing Social Media Burnout." *Nonprofit Tech 2.0.* October 22, 2009. http://nonprofitorgs.wordpress.com/2009/10/22/10-tips-for -managing-social-media-burnout/.

McConnell, Ben. "Crisis 101: now measured in minutes." *Church of the Customer Blog.* April 16, 2009. www.churchofcustomer.com/2009/04/crisis-101.html.

———. "The Last Temptation of Twitter." *Church of the Customer Blog.* December 19, 2008. www.churchofcustomer.com/2008/12/an-8020-rule-for-selfpromotion.html.

Merrill, Mike D. "Why Every Employee is a Salesperson—The Power of Social Media." July 27, 2009. http://mikemerrill.com/wordpress/2009/07/why-every-employee-is-a -salesperson-the-power-of-social-media/.

Moore-Jones, Michael. "Why Teens Don't and Won't Tweet." *ReadWriteWeb.* December 8, 2010. www.readwriteweb.com/archives/why_teens_dont_and_wont_tweet.php.

Morejon, Roy. "Social Media Age Demographics for Facebook and Twitter." August 30, 2011. http://roymorejon.com/social-media-age-demographics-for-facebook-and -twitter/.

Morrissey, Brian. "Who's in Charge of Social Media?" *Adweek.* October 19, 2009. www .adweek.com/news/technology/whos-charge-social-media-100647.

Nelson, Shannon. "Improving Brand Value through Social Media: Zappos Gets It Right," May 15, 2008. www.piercemattiepublicrelations.com/social_networks/.

Notter, Jamie. "Is Your Organization Human Enough for Social Media?" *SocialFish.* November 30, 2009. www.socialfish.org/2009/11/human-enough.html.

O'Dell, Jolie. "6 Challenges to Managing a Brand on the Social Web." *Mashable Social Media.* June 30, 2010. http://mashable.com/2010/06/30/brands-social-web/.

Ogneva, Maria. "Why You Need to Monitor and Measure Your Brand on Social Media." *Mashable Social Media.* July 29, 2010. http://mashable.com/2010/07/29/monitor -measure-brand-social-media/.

Ostrow, Adam. "Half of Social Media Users Connect With Brands." *Mashable Social Media.* August 31, 2009. http://mashable.com/2009/08/31/social-media-brands/.

———. "Hey, Teens: Your Parents Are Probably Checking Your Facebook [STUDY]." *Mashable Social Media.* October 20, 2010. http://mashable.com/2010/10/20/parents -teens-facebook-monitoring/.

Owyang, Jeremiah. "Build Your Network Before You Need Them." June 12, 2008. www .web-strategist.com/blog/2008/06/12/build-your-network-before-you-need-them/.

Pigott, Ike. "How to be a Social Media Advocate in Conservative Corporate Cultures." *SlideShare.* May 14, 2009. www.slideshare.net/ikepigott/how-to-be-a-social-media -advocate-in.

Pingdom. "Study: Ages of social network users." February 16, 2010. http://royal.pingdom .com/2010/02/16/study-ages-of-social-network-users/.

———. "Study: Males vs. females in social networks." November 27, 2009. http://royal .pingdom.com/2009/11/27/study-males-vs-females-in-social-networks/.

Pistorio, Yvette. "5 Twitter Mistakes to Avoid," June 30, 2011. http://blog.us.cision .com/2011/06/5-twitter-mistakes-to-avoid/.

Porterfield, Amy. "The 'Cool Kids' Strategy to Social Media Marketing." November 10, 2009. http://amyporterfield.com/index.php/2009/11/the-cool-kids-strategy-to-social-media-marketing/.

Probst, Mark R. "Amazon Follies." April 12, 2009. http://markprobst.livejournal.com/15293.html.

Purcell, Kristin, and Amanda Lenhart. "Trends in Teen Communication: Opportunities and Challenges for Public Health Campaigns." *Pew Internet.* September 29, 2010. http://pewinternet.com/Presentations/2010/Sep/ONDCP.aspx.

Qualman, Erik. *Socialnomics: How Social Media Transforms the Way We Live and Do Business.* Hoboken, NJ: John Wiley & Sons, 2009.

Randall, Kim. "How You Use Social Media Says A Lot About You and Your Brand." *Not Just Another Blog.* 2009. www.kimrandall.me/how-you-use-social-media-says-a-lot-about-you-and-your-brand/.

Rhodes, Matt. "Learn from Abercrombie & Fitch: Embed social media in every customer touchpoint." *Fresh Networks.* August 8, 2010. www.freshnetworks.com/blog/2010/08/abercrombie-fitch-social-media-strategy-customer-touchpoints/.

Robbins, Renee. "7 Creative Ways to Introduce Social Media to Your Team." October 22, 2009. www.evernote.com/shard/s6/note/b8a5ac0e-2abb-4eb0-a003-81ed60a9a738/rmegan/VirtuallyMeg#b=bd04db7f-042a-497f-b838-2ca5809c895c&n=b8a5ac0e-2abb-4eb0-a003-81ed60a9a738.

Robles, Patricio. "How do you handle feedback?" October 2, 2009 (10:59 a.m.). http://econsultancy.com/blog/4705-how-do-you-handle-feedback.

Rogers-Urbanek, Jenica P. *Going Beyond the Great Idea: Getting buy-in and doing effective training for 2.0 projects.* 2008. www2.potsdam.edu/rogersjp/CiL2008Acad2.0.pdf.

Ross, Joshua-Michéle. "Why Social Media Isn't for Everyone." *Mashable Social Media.* January 18, 2010. http://mashable.com/2010/01/18/social-media-not-for-everyone/.

Schaefer, Mark W. "How Social Media Can Hurt Business Relationships." December 20, 2009. http://businessesgrow.com/2009/12/20/how-social-media-can-hurt-business-relationships/.

Schawbel, Dan. "HOW TO: Build Your Personal Brand on Twitter." *Mashable Social Media.* May 20, 2009. http://mashable.com/2009/05/20/twitter-personal-brand/.

———. *Me 2.0: 4 Steps to Building Your Future.* Revised and updated ed. New York: Kaplan Publishing, 2010.

Shankman, Peter. "I Will Never Hire a 'Social Media Expert,' and Neither Should You." May 20, 2011. http://shankman.com/i-will-never-hire-a-social-media-expert-and-neither-should-you/.

Sherman, Aliza. "5 Things That Don't Work on Facebook Pages (and 5 That Do)." *GigaOm Web Worker Daily.* March 31, 2010. http://gigaom.com/collaboration/5-things-that-dont-work-on-facebook-pages-and-5-that-do/.

———. "6 Tips for Better Branding Using Avatars." *GigaOm Web Worker Daily.* July 16, 2009 (1:00 p.m.). http://gigaom.com/collaboration/6-tips-for-better-branding-using-avatars/.

———. "The Reluctant Social Media Client." *GigaOm Web Worker Daily.* November 21, 2008 (3:00 p.m.). http://gigaom.com/collaboration/the-reluctant-social-media-client/.

————. "The Value of Twitter Followers: Quality Over Quantity." *GigaOm Web Worker Daily*. July 2, 2009 (1:00 p.m.). http://gigaom.com/collaboration/the-value-of-twitter-followers-quality-over-quantity/.

————. "Why Should I Engage in Social Media?" *GigaOm Web Worker Daily*. September 28, 2009 (7:00 a.m.). http://gigaom.com/collaboration/why-should-i-engage-in-social-media-for-business/.

Shields, Mike. "Young Users Hating on Brands." *Adweek*. March 9, 2011. www.adweek.com/news/advertising-branding/young-users-hating-brands-126346.

Smith, Mari. "10 Tips for Creating Buzz with Facebook Events." *Social Media Examiner*. October 29, 2009. www.socialmediaexaminer.com/10-tips-for-creating-buzz-with-facebook-events/.

————. "Social Media Success—15 Hot Tips From The Pied Piper!" August 12, 2009. www.marismith.com/social-media-success-15-hot-tips-from-the-pied-piper/.

Sniderman, Zachary. "5 Ways to Clean Up Your Social Media Identity." *Mashable Social Media*. July 6, 2010. http://mashable.com/2010/07/06/clean-social-media-identity/.

Solis, Brian. *Engage! The Complete Guide for Brands and Businesses to Build, Cultivate, and Measure Success in the New Web*. Hoboken, NJ: John Wiley & Sons, 2011.

————. "The Maturation of Social Media ROI." *Mashable Social Media*. January 26, 2010. http://mashable.com/2010/01/26/maturation-social-media-roi/.

————. "What IF We Redefined Influence? The New Influence Factor in Social Media." November 11, 2009. www.briansolis.com/2009/11/what-if-we-redefined-influence-the-evolution-of-the-influence-factor-in-social-media/?success.

Spiro, Josh. "A New Source of Stress: Feelings of Social Media Inadequacy." *Inc*. December 10, 2009. www.inc.com/news/articles/2009/12/afraid-of-social-media.html.

Staib, Karl. "14 Ways to Fight Twitter Burnout." *TwiTip*. November 20, 2009. www.twitip.com/14-ways-to-fight-twitter-burnout/.

Strickland, Marta. "How to Do Social Media Right in 2009." *SlideShare*. March 14, 2009. www.slideshare.net/mstrickland/how-to-do-social-media-right-in-2009.

Sukernek, Warren. "@HiltonAnaheim—There's more to Twitter than broadcasting your ads." *Twittermaven*. December 28, 2009. twittermaven.blogspot.com/2009/12/hiltonanaheim-theres-more-to-twitter.html.

Sutter, John D. "Ashton Kutcher challenges CNN to Twitter popularity contest." *CNN.com*. April 15, 2009. www.cnn.com/2009/TECH/04/15/ashton.cnn.twitter.battle/index.html.

Sutton, Wayne. "7 Habits of Highly Effective Twitterers." May 21, 2009 (6:22 p.m.). http://blog.mrtweet.net/7-habits-of-highly-effective-twitterers-wayne-sutton.

Titlow, John Paul. "Despite Living Online, Teenagers Don't Want to 'Like' Your Company on Facebook." *ReadWriteWeb*. March 8, 2011. www.readwriteweb.com/biz/2011/03/despite-living-online-teenagers-dont-like-companies-on-facebook.php.

————. "How to Convert a Facebook Profile to a Page." *ReadWriteWeb*. March 10, 2011. www.readwriteweb.com/biz/2011/03/how-to-convert-a-facebook-profile-to-a-page.php.

Thompson, Clive. "Clive Thompson in Praise of Online Obscurity." *Wired*. January 25, 2010. www.wired.com/magazine/2010/01/st_thompson_obscurity.

———. "Clive Thompson on Secret Messages in the Digital Age." *Wired*. January 2011. www.wired.com/magazine/2011/01/st_thompson_secretmessages/.

Trapani, Gina. "Information Overload is Filter Failure, Says Shirky." *Lifehacker Australia*. September 22, 2008. www.lifehacker.com.au/2008/09/information_overload_is_filter_failure_says_shirky-2/.

Tsotsis, Alexa. "What Do Teens Want? Their Moms Off Facebook." *SF Weekly*. October 22, 2009. http://blogs.sfweekly.com/shookdown/2009/10/what_do_teens_want.php.

Twittown. "Five Wickedly Clever Ways to Use Twitter." October 26, 2009. http://twittown .com/social-networks/social-networks-blog/five-wickedly-clever-ways-use-twitter.

Uhrmacher, Aaron. "How to Measure Social Media ROI for Business." *Mashable Social Media*. July 31, 2008. http://mashable.com/2008/07/31/measuring-social-media-roi -for-business/.

Van Grove, Jennifer. "19% of Internet Users Now Use Status Updates." *Mashable Social Media*. October 21, 2009. http://mashable.com/2009/10/21/pew-september-data/.

———. "Teens Experiencing Facebook Fatigue [STUDY]." *Mashable Social Media*. June 30, 2010. http://mashable.com/2010/06/30/teens-social-networks-study/.

———. "What Social Media Users Want." *Mashable Social Media*. March 18, 2010. http:// mashable.com/2010/03/18/social-media-sites-data/.

Waddell, Darren. "Social Marketing Continues Meteoric Rise among Local Businesses." *MerchantCircle Press Releases*. February 15, 2011. www.merchantcircle.com/corporate/ press/2011-01-15-social-marketing-continues-meteoric-rise-among-local-businesses .html.

Walter, Ekaterina. "10 Tips for Posting on Your Brand's Facebook Page." *Mashable Social Media*. March 22, 2011. http://mashable.com/2011/03/22/tips-brand-facebook-page/.

Warren, Christina. "HOW TO: Measure Social Media ROI." *Mashable Social Media*. October 27, 2009. http://mashable.com/2009/10/27/social-media-roi/.

West, Jessamyn. "Library of Congress reports on Flickr project." *librarian.net*. December 14, 2008. www.librarian.net/stax/2607/library-of-congress-reports-on-flickr-project/.

Williams, Alex. "Study: Enterprise Lags in Social Web Savviness." *ReadWriteWeb*. October 7, 2009. www.readwriteweb.com/enterprise/2009/10/deloitte-study-shows-the-enter .php.

Worthington, Paul. "How to Be Generous: A Guide for Social Media Brands." *Mashable Social Media*. June 18, 2009. http://mashable.com/2009/06/18/social-media-generosity/.

Yared, Peter. "Why Most Facebook Marketing Doesn't Work." *ReadWriteWeb*. February 17, 2011. www.readwriteweb.com/archives/why_most_facebook_marketing_doesnt_ work.php.

INDEX

Locators in **bold** refer to figures/tables

You may also be interested in

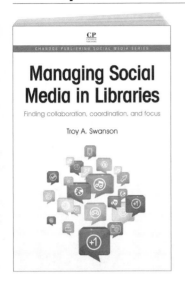

MANAGING SOCIAL MEDIA IN LIBRARIES
FINDING COLLABORATION, COORDINATION, AND FOCUS
Troy A. Swanson

This book shows library managers and leaders ways social media can strengthen connections between the library and its users.

ISBN: 978-1-8433-4711-8
194 pp / 6" × 9"

BUILDING A BUZZ
PEGGY BARBER,
LINDA WALLACE
ISBN: 978-0-8389-1011-5

BITE-SIZED MARKETING
NANCY DOWD,
MARY EVANGELISTE,
JONATHAN SILBERMAN
ISBN: 978-0-8389-1000-9

SMALL PUBLIC LIBRARY MANAGEMENT
JANE PEARLMUTTER,
PAUL NELSON
ISBN: 978-0-8389-1085-6

GOOGLE THIS! PUTTING GOOGLE AND OTHER SOCIAL MEDIA SITES TO WORK FOR YOUR LIBRARY
TERRY BALLARD
ISBN: 978-1-8433-4677-7

BRIDGING THE DIGITAL DIVIDE WITH MOBILE SERVICES
ANDROMEDA YELTON
ISBN: 978-0-8389-5856-8

DOING SOCIAL MEDIA SO IT MATTERS: A LIBRARIAN'S GUIDE
LAURA SOLOMON
ISBN: 978-0-8389-1067-2

Order today at **alastore.ala.org** or **866-746-7252!**
ALA Store purchases fund advocacy, awareness, and accreditation programs for library professionals worldwide.